The Secret of
The Alchemist

Colm Holland

The Secret of
The Alchemist

Colm Holland

BOOKS

Winchester, UK
Washington, USA

JOHN HUNT PUBLISHING

First published by O-Books, 2020
O-Books is an imprint of John Hunt Publishing Ltd., 3 East St., Alresford,
Hampshire SO24 9EE, UK
office@jhpbooks.com
www.johnhuntpublishing.com
www.o-books.com

For distributor details and how to order please visit the 'Ordering' section on our website.

Text copyright: Colm Holland 2019
Cover image Copyright: Colm Holland 2019

ISBN: 978 1 78904 434 8
978 1 78904 435 5 (ebook)
Library of Congress Control Number: 2019945253

A CIP catalogue record for this book is available from the British Library.

(All biblical references are from the King James Bible, 1611.)

Professional Services Disclaimer
Neither the author nor the publisher is engaged in rendering professional services to the
reader and shall not be liable or responsible for any loss or damage allegedly arising from
any information or suggestions in this book. The ideas, procedures and suggestions contained
therein are not intended as a substitute for consulting with a qualified physician or professional
financial advisor. Further, the publisher and author assume no responsibility for the content of
third party books or websites recommended in this book.

Design: Stuart Davies

UK: Printed and bound by CPI Group (UK) Ltd, Croydon, CR0 4YY
Printed in North America by CPI GPS partners

We operate a distinctive and ethical publishing philosophy in
all areas of our business, from our global network of authors to
production and worldwide distribution.

Contents

To my wife and lifelong soulmate. I am blessed they are one and the same person.

To my kids who now realize they are wiser than me.

To my grandkids who have the opportunity to learn from my mistakes.

To all those who have loved me unconditionally, and to those who have not.

To all those whose immense generosity I have been privileged to receive.

To all who hunger and thirst for the answers to a meaningful life.

To Love in them all.

With a special dedication to the memory of Dr. Frank Lake (1914–1982), the founder of Clinical Theology.

'The greatest challenge we face is to truly believe, at the very core of our heart, we are loved unconditionally for who we are, and not for what we can do.'
Colm Holland

Preface

My Encounter with *The Alchemist*

In 1993, I was a member of the international marketing team at one of the world's leading publishers in Australia. On Friday of every week, I received a pile of manuscripts in the mail from our editorial department in San Francisco. It was my job to review and decide which upcoming books we should distribute "down under."

These books were part of our New Age list, and back then there was only a fledgling market for these in Australian bookshops. The bestsellers of the day were mostly sports biographies, gruesome crime fiction, action thrillers and racy romance novels. How times have changed.

In one such pile of esoteric manuscripts, I was struck by the cover art of a title called *The Alchemist*, a novel by Paulo Coelho, who at the time was an unknown Brazilian author. The notes to the book explained that this was the first English translation of the original Portuguese text. The cover design was a strikingly colorful and naive drawing of a one-eyed figure in traditional Arabian dress and a young pilgrim, against a purple background. I instantly found it mesmerizing. So much so that I broke my rule of not taking work home at the weekend and slipped the manuscript into my briefcase as I closed the door on another long week in my office.

It was after lunch on Sunday afternoon when I remembered the manuscript. I set myself up on my garden chair, under the shade of a large gum tree in our backyard at home in Sydney, to read a few pages.

The sun set and the light faded on the final page of the manuscript as I completed the read in one sitting. There was no doubt in my mind; I had just read a book that would become an

1

international bestseller!

Here was a simple story of a young shepherd named Santiago who is able to find a treasure beyond his wildest dreams. Along the way he learns to listen to his heart, and, more importantly, realizes that his dreams are not just his but part of the "soul of the world."

The following Monday I was on the phone to my colleague in California, waking him at home at seven o'clock in the morning.

"Hi, Colm," he muttered. "It's great to hear from you, but can't it wait at least until after I've had my first coffee?"

"Tell me more about Paulo Coelho." I ignored his pleas for consideration. I was convinced we were sitting on a once-in-a-lifetime literary phenomenon.

My colleague turned on his coffee grinder, and over the noise he began to explain that Paulo was a well-known author in Brazil. His books were in Portuguese, and *The Alchemist* was a local success. Our firm had bought the world rights.

"The plan is to release a small print run in hardcover and see how the English language market responds," he explained. "How many do you want? Two hundred or three hundred copies?" He was used to those sorts of numbers from Australia.

Without hesitation I told him, "I want twenty thousand copies in paperback and a backup print run of at least thirty thousand ready for when that sells out."

I could hear him gasp and half choke on a mouthful of coffee.

"Colm, are you serious?"

"You've read the book. You know I'm right!"

"OK, I'll see what the rest of the English-speaking territory thinks of your assessment. Now hang up and let me take a shower, or I'll be late for the office!"

My colleague had published hundreds of books and was skeptical of outlandish sales predictions and print runs. Publishers quickly lose money from that sort of unreasoned behavior. However, he was a man of his word. He called me back three days later and said we were going to print one hundred thousand copies — and that most of my global colleagues agreed with me that this book had a great chance of selling well.

Within the first month of publication, the entire quantity had sold out of the bookstores and has since gone one on to sell over eighty-five million copies worldwide. It has been translated into more than seventy languages and remained on the New York Times bestseller list for years after its initial publication. Paulo has more than twenty-nine million Facebook followers and fifteen million Twitter followers.

Like millions of people, including broadcaster Oprah Winfrey, President Bill Clinton, actor Will Smith and more recently the singer Pharrell Williams, *The Alchemist* has influenced my life. For me, the influence came not just from reading the book but from meeting its author.

Paulo Coelho had become an overnight literary sensation across the world. In Australia, soon after publication, he received his first English language review and was invited to keynote at the annual Adelaide Writers' Festival, where he was greeted with huge acclaim. On his way home to Brazil, Paulo and his wife Christina stopped by Sydney and graciously invited Naomi, our head of publicity, along with me and our respective partners to a thank-you meal.

I was excited for two reasons. It was only the second time in my career that an author had taken the trouble to thank me like this personally, and to spend time with such a creative spirit was an unmissable opportunity.

"Where are we meeting tonight, and how many are going?" I asked Naomi, as I stuck my head inside her office the afternoon of the meal.

"I've booked the Waterfront for 8 PM, and it's just the four of us with Paulo and his wife. He said to book the best restaurant in town." Naomi smiled.

"Wow! That's very generous." I was especially pleased there

would only be a small group of us. So often, author dinners were dominated by a host of must-be-invited company executives.

"And Paulo said he has a surprise for us both," Naomi said with a wink.

My sense of anticipation was growing by the second. "I can't wait. See you there!"

The evening was everything I had hoped for. The six of us chatted and shared stories together over a wonderful meal as if we were lifelong friends. Paulo was a warm hearted and generous host and obviously in love with his wife, Christina. He took a genuine interest in each of us, asking about our families, our hopes and aspirations. The three hours flew by, and I was sad when things started to draw to a close. I had completely forgotten about the surprise Naomi had mentioned.

"Before we all depart, I want to express my sincere thanks to my two new friends, Naomi and Colm," Paulo said as he reached inside his jacket for a small gift-wrapped box.

He placed the present in front of Naomi. "This," he exclaimed, "is a small token of thanks for all the care and attention you gave me and Christina in Adelaide this week and for the wonderful press coverage you have generated for me this year in Australia. I asked God, and Christina, what you would like. I hope they got it right." He smiled his famous boyish grin.

For once Naomi was speechless and I detected a tear in her eye. The table was silent as she carefully unwrapped the box to reveal an amazing diamond dress ring. She was genuinely shocked and as she struggled to hold back her emotions, it seemed exactly what she would have wanted. Naomi was one of the best publicity managers I have ever worked with. She went the second mile on a regular basis for all her authors. It was as if Paulo's gift was given on behalf of the hundreds who had failed to say thanks so generously. We all broke into spontaneous applause.

I was shaken out of my joy for Naomi by Paulo's voice, which

I suddenly realized was directed at me.

"Colm, what can I say?" His words hung in the air. His smile turned to a more serious look as he continued. "I heard about that early morning phone call you made to California, and the belief you placed in my book. If you'd not done that, we would not be sitting here tonight. I was unknown outside Brazil and you helped to change that. For this I will always be grateful."

Now it was my turn to be speechless. When I made that call to California, I had believed I was simply doing my job and that this truly was a great book. I also knew that others would agree with my judgment and, without feeling smug, it was good to know I had been right.

"Thanks, Paulo," I finally managed to say, "but I can't take credit for the fact that you wrote a wonderful book."

"Even so, Colm, you caught the vision of what I had written, and so I have asked God how I could thank you."

Now he had me guessing. I caught my wife's eye and she looked as clueless as I felt while we waited to hear God's answer. Would he reach into his jacket a second time and produce a mystery gift?

Paulo's focus was unchanged as he continued to look me in the eyes. "I've spent many hours asking God what I should give you, and I was told to spend a whole day of my time to call on the universe to give you everything you need to become the alchemist in your world, so that whatever you want will come to pass."

He paused for a moment as if he was recalling the miracle he had performed. He continued, "All you need is to decide what you want."

He fell silent and it was as if something tangible and yet invisible had been called into being right there at the table. I had no doubt we had just witnessed a moment of true sincerity which was infinitely more valuable than any material gift. Almost, dare I say, as if God had just spoken.

Paulo broke the mystical moment he had just created. He stood and began to shake our hands and said they must be going, early flights to catch and thanks for a wonderful evening all round; and he was gone.

I was in a daze. We congratulated Naomi on her beautiful ring and made our way home. As we drove along the freeway, I remember asking my wife what she thought about what Paulo had said. She wisely replied, "It doesn't matter what I think, it's what you think that counts."

And that was the problem. At that moment I had no idea what I thought, except that something completely unique had just taken place. What if Paulo was right? What if he had performed a miracle on my behalf, and the universe would give me everything I needed to achieve whatever I wanted?

My very next thought was, "What do I really want in my life?"

The answer came instantly, from deep within my soul.

"I want to fulfill all my dreams!"

In this book I will reveal *The Secret of The Alchemist* and how by applying it I have seen my life transformed and my dreams fulfilled.

Acknowledgements

This book would not exist unless Paulo Coelho had written *The Alchemist*, which was published in English by HarperCollins in 1993. And so I must first and foremost thank him for his gift to the world. The impact his book has made on my life, and my meeting with him, is mostly what this book is all about, and I have told the story of our initial meeting in my preface.

Thanks must go to my editor, Laurie Devine, an award-winning fiction author of several international bestsellers. Laurie has been a professional mentor and a source of great encouragement from our very first meeting.

Thanks are due to those whose stories I have told. Their names and details have been changed to protect their privacy, but they know who they are and they know how grateful I am for their consent in letting me share their experiences.

The cover illustration is a unique artwork that has pride of place in my office and has been an inspiration to me throughout. When you read this book, you will discover the artist who created it, and she has my deepest gratitude for sharing her creative spirit.

Thanks to John Hunt Publishing for bringing this book into being.

Finally, my thanks to my amazing wife and family. Their love and commitment to me is woven into the story of my life, and without them I would not be who I am today. They embody the unconditional love that has inspired me to write this book.

Colm Holland, 2019.

Author's note

I am conscious that we all bring our own meaning and understanding to a word. A single word can be packed with different intellectual and emotional connotations for each of us: often helpful and sometimes not. This book is not an attempt to redefine the meaning of any word. But I do want you, the reader, to be clear about the understanding I have of one of the most common words in the world. I refer throughout this book to Love.

Love is a word with multiple meanings in many languages, and perhaps most of all in English because we use it in many unconnected contexts, from sexual attraction to simply liking an object.

My use of the word Love in *The Secret of The Alchemist* carries a very specific meaning and for that reason I am giving it a capital L throughout. I am referring to unconditional Love.

This is a Love that cares beyond measure, never gives up, constantly wants the best for another, forgives and never judges, is full of compassion and mercy, and feels the pain and joy of others deeply. It is a Love revealed through action. This is my definition of Love, and it has no bounds and is unchanging.

Love is also the name I give to the force that exists within the very fabric of all life and across the cosmos; it holds all things together and is what I constantly seek to become one with, so I, too, can Love unconditionally.

This Love will give you what you want, if you let it.

Introduction

"Why is Paulo Coelho's book, *The Alchemist,* so popular around the world?" I asked myself during the time when the book was first published and then quickly hit *The New York Times* bestseller list. As each of the twenty-five years have passed since that first afternoon when I was alone with the original manuscript, I have been amazed how my prediction that this book would be a bestseller has been fulfilled beyond my wildest expectations. For quite a while Paulo held the Guinness World Record for the most translations of a single title by a living author, beaten only recently by *Harry Potter and the Philosopher's Stone.* My enduring question has been, "What is it about the story of Santiago that has captured so many readers' hearts?"

Is *The Alchemist* so successful because of its simple message: follow your dreams and you will find them? Or are there other, more significant factors within the story? Why has the book seen such a universal appeal across all cultures? Are there hidden secrets just waiting to be discovered? If there are, I thought, I will make it my mission to find them, so I can benefit from their power to turn all my dreams into reality.

Before I go any further with this introduction, I am aware that you are probably wondering what happened after my meeting with Paulo Coelho as I described in the preface. I will finish that story so you can fully understand why I wrote this book.

By the time my wife and I arrived home and fell into bed that night, I had begun to wonder why Paulo had not simply produced an expensive men's fashion watch from his other jacket pocket. At least then, I thought, I would have something tangible to show for his gratitude. The significance and the magnitude of what Paulo said he had done on my behalf faded as I wearily considered all the demands of work the next day, and then drifted off to sleep.

Back at the office the following morning, I heard one of my colleagues shriek with delight when she saw Naomi's new expensive ring. Then that same woman stuck her head into my office to ask the inevitable question. What did Paulo give me? When I gave her my "don't even ask" glare, she smiled uncertainly and beat a hasty retreat.

I joked later with Naomi that I did not have a watch to show off.

"You should be careful." She laughed. "You may just get what you wish for. Isn't that what Paulo said? But to be honest, I've never taken you to be a bling jewelry kind of guy."

I laughed and made an excuse to get back to work as I absorbed the impact of what she had said. "You may just get what you wish for." She was right, jewelry was not one of my priorities in life. Yet somehow I passed off her comments without another thought. At that moment my only wish was to get through all the responsibilities of my day-to-day work, as uninspiring as that prospect was.

The truth is I felt trapped in that middle-management treadmill so often experienced by anyone working in a corporate environment. I felt underpaid and underappreciated, with no way out. More importantly, I had begun to realize I had lost my enthusiasm and passion for what I was doing. I had a family to support and needed the money, just like millions of others who toil daily in jobs where they do not feel fulfilled. To compound the situation, I had two senior executives I reported to whose management styles not only made it difficult for me and others to do their job well, but also took all the fun out of it.

My underlying but unstated desire at the moment I met Paulo was to leave corporate life and start my own business. I just needed the courage and the opportunity to make the break without, for my family's sake, putting my financial future at risk. What I still lacked was the sense of empowerment to take the risk and make the move.

So, what did happen next?

I started to listen to my heart. It told me, if I studied *The Alchemist* in depth to find the secret of its success, I would indeed discover how to achieve all my dreams.

Paulo had ignited my rational curiosity to the point where I began to constantly wonder whether there might be something in his book I was missing. Maybe there were concealed and powerful truths lying within that story; if I could find them, then perhaps miracles would happen for me.

I am excited to say that as I studied the book, I did indeed discover its "secret," and as I applied it to my life, miracles did begin to happen. In fact, they happened almost immediately. The two executives who were blocks to my progress in the company were fired and went on to even better jobs in another company. Then, surprisingly—to me, anyway—I was promoted to an executive position. I was so amazed by this sudden turn of good fortune that I continued to apply what I had discovered in *The Alchemist.* Within a year I found the courage to leave corporate life and start my own business, just as I had dreamed. Again, incredibly, the company I started became the most successful independent digital marketing agency in Australia at that time! Finally, seven years after first reading *The Alchemist* and applying its secret to my life, I left my marketing career and dedicated my time to sharing with others the knowledge that transformed my life.

I'm sure you will agree that owning a gold wristwatch pales into insignificance compared with the success I achieved in my career and the new purpose I found. Even more importantly, I want to share with you how, by discovering *The Secret of The Alchemist,* we can find true empowerment and perform amazing miracles.

I will explain how a life of powerlessness can be transformed into a life of passion, enthusiasm, joy, fulfillment and gold.

I made the final decision to write this book just over a year ago, in 2017, when I was browsing for children's books with my four-year-old grandson in a small, secondhand bookshop. While I was helping him choose a book, I gave into a strong impulse to ask the bookseller if she had *The Alchemist* in stock, even though I had a copy at home.

"Well, that's a coincidence," she said. "Only yesterday someone brought in an old copy. Let me see." She reached to a shelf behind her and took down a well-worn copy of *The Alchemist*. She handed me the book. I smiled as I read the inscription someone had written on the first page:

"We are all alchemists, as we try to find the formula for our life!"

I had long ago stopped believing in coincidences and knew I had already discovered the most powerful formula anyone could imagine, thanks to *The Alchemist*. I decided it was time to reveal it to the world at large.

I bought that preloved copy of the book to mark the occasion of my decision. As I paid the bookseller, I noted that my grandson had chosen, *Oh, the Places You'll Go*, by Dr. Seuss.

I smiled at his choice: this was surely another omen to begin writing this book.

Within a week of that decision, I spotted a lady behind me on a flight reading *The Alchemist*. Then, two days later, someone reading it on an underground train in London, and the next day a young woman with a copy in a hotel lobby where I was staying. Coincidences? No! Of course not! Remember, this was twenty-five years after *The Alchemist* was first published in English; and before this, in my daily comings and goings, I had rarely seen a copy being read in public. Not that I needed further endorsement of my decision, yet I took this as another omen that Love was encouraging me to reveal *The Secret of The Alchemist*.

This book is not an autobiography. It's the revelation of how I discovered *The Secret of The Alchemist* and how, by following the insights I have discerned, you can perform miracles in your life.

I have no doubt that Love has actively encouraged and aided me in writing this book for the reasons you will discover as you read on. My core aim is to assist you in your own quest for a life full of power to change your world.

In chapter one I will outline what I believe true empowerment is and what it can look like in your life. Then I will reveal *The Secret of The Alchemist* and how it can be a force for positive change. As you read each chapter, the insights needed to discover true empowerment will be revealed. The full power lies in all the insights combined, but one of the most exciting things about *The Secret of The Alchemist* is you do not have to wait for the final insight to see new power develop. In fact, the moment you begin this book you will see an improvement in your personal power if you really want it. As you complete this book and apply each insight, you will be able to create everything you need to live a life full of positivity, compassion, purpose and miracles.

How do I know? This is a promise I am making to you: I have asked Love to give you everything you need, so that whatever you want will come to pass. All you need is to decide what you want.

Welcome to *The Secret of The Alchemist*.

Chapter 1

True Empowerment

True empowerment through transformation is my consuming passion, and sharing it is my life's mission. I will define what I mean by true empowerment and transformation shortly, and we will see why I'm obsessed with the subject as we discover its miraculous potential for the better in every aspect of our lives.

To help explain what true empowerment looks like, I want to tell a real story. It is one of my all-time favorites because it encompasses at every level the key manifestations of what true empowerment through transformation can be, and I was also fortunate to be present when it reached its wonderful climax.

Victoria's Story

In a large Australian publishing house, Victoria was an assistant to Penny, one of the most demanding and, unfortunately, unappreciative publishers in the firm. Although Victoria was very successful in her job, one of Penny's key missions in life seemed to be giving Victoria the most thankless and laborious tasks she could find, and then taking all the credit with the firm's executives for any good work.

As you can imagine, Victoria was growing increasingly frustrated in her job and wished for a different life, where she followed her true talent and would feel fulfilled and enthusiastic. Herein lay the problem. She had no idea what her true talent was. Her life so far had consisted of school, college, work, raising a family and more work. She had devoted the best years of her life to raising her kids and was immensely proud of them and their achievements. She was in a happy marriage with plenty of wonderful friends and a full social life. But at this point her creative soul was asking, "What about me? When do I get to express myself?"

I also distinctly remember her asking, "What is the thing I have yet to discover that will release my creativity? I feel this deep need to express my inner self, to be fulfilled, but I have no idea what that would look like. Maybe I should help people by learning Swedish massage? I just don't know. The one thing I do know is that my inner fulfillment is not about making Penny look good at my expense!"

Victoria heard about my encounter with *The Alchemist* and had seen firsthand how dramatically my life had changed for the better. She told me she wanted to know *The Secret of The Alchemist*. I explained what I had discovered and she started to apply the insights I have outlined in this book. Most importantly, she began by asking Love to reveal her "thing."

A few months after our conversation, Penny gave Victoria the painstaking task of sorting and cataloging boxes and boxes of old photographic transparencies of the work of Australian artists. Over the years these treasures had been used in a multitude of beautiful coffee table books which represented the entire history of great Australian fine art, both Aboriginal and European.

"I nearly died when I saw the size of the task," she told me at the time. "The transparencies were in no order at all. Some were labelled with the name of the artist and the book they were in, but most were not." This meant she had to discover in which of these many books each transparency had appeared, and then label them with the artist, title and relevant date. The project turned into three months of painstaking work, on top of her role as Penny's personal assistant.

Victoria later recalled her feelings. "I was depressed just at the thought of the unreasonable request Penny was making and even more discouraged by my inability to say no. This was definitely not in my job description."

The situation made Victoria angry at several levels. She felt a genuine resentment toward Penny, while struggling to find her own power in the situation and was not willing to accept feeling victimized by her circumstances.

Then a miracle happened. As she began to apply *The Secret of The Alchemist*, and at the same time was laboring day after day with cataloging those photographs, something was ignited within that she could never have predicted.

"As I worked my way through transparency after transparency," she told me, "my appreciation of the great artists and their work grew daily. Their amazing art began to feed my soul, and in the solitude of the task I felt a connection with these talented spirits. My eyes were opened to a whole new world of artistic creativity, and it was then I realized what my "thing" was. I wanted to express myself through painting!"

What had been a daunting everyday dread became her passion. She was now able to throw herself into the task with enthusiasm and joy. Ironically, as she immersed herself in the artists' styles and individual techniques, she was becoming an expert on Australian fine art.

Then another unexpected event took place. Her husband got a new job with double the pay. Because he had seen Victoria's love of art blossom, he encouraged her to leave fulltime work and take professional art classes.

"My response to his offer was not what I expected," she told me. "Instead of excitement, I felt a new fear. Did I believe I actually had the talent? What if I was simply not that good at it?"

Past feelings of not being affirmed suddenly emerged. Growing up, her parents and teachers had not encouraged her to develop her creative skills. If she was going to finally find fulfilment, she had to summon all her courage, believe in herself and make a leap of faith. She decided, just as she was completing the assignment, to resign and step out into the unknown. She was going to take up painting.

Just a few years later, Victoria invited me to the reception party of the annual National Australian Art Exhibition and

Awards. Every year thousands of artists enter their work in the hope of being named the landscape or portrait artist of the year. It is a big deal, and only a few of the very best finalists are exhibited. This was the first time Victoria had entered one of her paintings. She swore me to secrecy that her work had made the final selection and would be in the exhibition.

For visitors this is the most attended yearly art exhibition in all of Australia. Even the announcement of winners makes the front page of the national press. The opening party is televised with a host of celebrities and national dignitaries present. I was invited because Victoria had given me this particular painting as a thank you for my previous help. But she had borrowed it back with the promise she would return it when the exhibition was over. I was flattered on all counts and arrived at the reception full of excitement. It was a red-carpet event, and I recognized some of the most famous contemporary Australian artists posing for the press photographers.

Victoria's landscape painting was one of only twenty-three chosen from thousands entered and would be on display in the art gallery for six weeks. Although Victoria was not the ultimate winner, she was overjoyed just to be in the exhibition and have her artistic talent on display to an audience of tens of thousands. Here she was, her work exhibited in the national gallery only a few years after feeling unfulfilled and powerless in her circumstances. Several times that evening I shared her delight as we walked around admiring the work of the other finalists.

It was at that moment, as incredible as it may sound, that I witnessed firsthand the true empowerment Victoria now possessed. As we turned a corner in the exhibition, standing with a group of the gallery's benefactors was Penny—Victoria's old boss. If I had not been a witness, I would still find it hard to believe what happened next.

Victoria and I both froze, and I saw Penny spot us and say out loud, "I don't believe it! Look who's here!" I saw the genuine expression of disbelief on her face as she approached us.

"Colm, what a pleasant surprise!" she exclaimed, and then she turned to Victoria with a quizzical look. "And, Victoria, what are *you* doing here?" Penny had to have known the opening VIP event was by invitation only.

It was obvious to us both that Penny had no idea that Victoria's painting was in the exhibition. I decided to have some fun.

"Hello, Penny," I said. "Try and have a guess why Victoria and I are here."

"Well, let me see!" Penny was in good spirits and seemed keen to enter into the game. She looked at me. "Colm, you're involved in promoting the event on the internet?"

I smiled. "Good guess, but not quite the right one. Do you want to try again?"

Penny was relishing the quiz we were playing, although she continued to ignore Victoria. "Your son's work is in the exhibition? If I remember right, he studied art?"

"Another close guess! Yes, he did, but that's not the answer! I'll give you one last chance." I turned my gaze toward Victoria.

Penny followed my gaze and stared at Victoria. I watched as her mind worked its way through the past preconceptions and prejudice she had exhibited toward her former assistant.

"Not Victoria! Are *you* in this exhibition?" Her scream was loud enough that others walked over to see what was going on.

I saw the biggest smile I had ever seen appear on Victoria's face as she said nothing and watched Penny come to terms with a new reality; her previous assistant, whom she had treated very shabbily, was now an accomplished and publicly recognized artist. This was a reality Victoria had created by using *The Secret of The Alchemist*. She had found the courage within to follow her heart. And she had been richly rewarded for stepping out into the unknown.

Penny and her group gathered around Victoria's painting with plenty of "Oohs!" and "Ahs!" of appreciation. I stepped back and watched Victoria enjoy the moment. Everyone wanted a photo taken with this new celebrity artist.

A quick postscript to this story. Penny announced to the group that she owed a debt of gratitude to Victoria when they worked together. "She saved my life at the firm," were the exact words, I recall. These were belated thanks and probably the nearest thing to an apology Penny was likely to offer for not expressing her gratitude to Victoria at the time.

I never did get that painting back because it sold to a collector for a considerable sum while in the exhibition, but I proudly have a similar version that Victoria gave me later. Her work is now collected around the world and has brought pleasure and inspiration to many.

My greatest reward from this story has been the knowledge that all the resentment and powerlessness Victoria felt at the time she worked with Penny had evaporated. A transformation had taken place. There they stood—more than equals—in that precious moment in the gallery. As they continued to talk, Victoria thanked Penny for giving her the task of cataloging all those artists, which had opened up her own desire to paint. Penny then confessed to Victoria that she had wanted to be an actress when she was young, that she'd had the talent but never had the courage to follow her dream. She added that later she at least had been able to watch her daughter become a professional actress, even though she missed the chance herself. Being a publisher, she admitted, had never been the fulfilling life's work she had hoped for.

I watched as Victoria reacted with grace and compassion for Penny; there and then, she encouraged her to rediscover her talent for acting. She inspired and empowered Penny to find her own true self.

* * *

True empowerment is an encompassing state of wellbeing. It is a condition of personal wholeness where the soul, mind and body are fully integrated and are at one with Love. It is a place of authenticity and truth. It is a place from which dreams and goals can be fulfilled unhindered. It is a manifestation of Love in all humankind and a vehicle by which change for the better is created. It is freely available to anyone who seeks the greater good beyond the realms of selfish desire. It is yours for the taking if you truly want it. It is the treasure you will find when you follow your true destiny. It is the ability to change your world for the better. How to achieve this true empowerment is revealed in *The Secret of The Alchemist,* and it is available to anyone who passionately wants it.

Transformation is the process we must pass through to reach true empowerment. It's not about trying to become someone other than who we really are. It's an inward journey toward discovering our true soul. It involves an inner catharsis toward wholeness rather than a striving for an unattainable state of perfection. It means valuing our frailty and woundedness and allowing Love to heal and restore the power of our unique individuality. It is about looking within so we can move forward to a place of true empowerment, where we can offer compassion, empathy and healing to everyone in our world. The starting point is right where we are now, and the process never fully ends because transformation becomes our new way of life. It is our friend, and we can embrace it without fear.

* * *

The story of Santiago, the main protagonist in *The Alchemist,* is at one level a simple tale of how to fulfill a dream. In the beginning his daily occupation is as a shepherd; his main focus is looking after his sheep, which are his livelihood.

However, he feels unfulfilled in this task and has a dream of discovering buried treasure, although he has no real idea of what that looks like. All he senses is that he must leave the safety and familiarity of his surroundings and venture into an unknown land. Along the way he meets several people who give him pointers to assist his search for the treasure. Most importantly, he finds the courage to overcome his fears and face various life-threatening dangers. He is empowered to follow his heart to the place of the pyramids, only to discover the treasure is back in the abandoned chapel where he first had his dream. He returns and discovers the gold.

This is the obvious theme on the surface of *The Alchemist*, and it is a powerful one. It is certainly the same theme running through Victoria's experience, and that of many people who have read *The Alchemist*, have been inspired to follow their dreams and discover their talents and gifts. This message is also not unique to *The Alchemist*. Literally hundreds of contemporary self-improvement books have a similar theme.

Follow your dreams. Listen to your heart. Face your fears. Learn from others. Stick to your goal. Believe you can do it. Make the good of others your aim. Do these things and you will find your true talents to use for your benefit and those in your world.

This is a universal truth and is the bedrock of how to find true empowerment.

However, even though I knew all this to be true, it still did not explain to me why *The Alchemist* had reached millions upon millions of reader's hearts when so many other books with a similar message must have had an equal chance of such success but did not achieve the same result?

That question motivated me to keep digging to find the secret still buried within the story. In the next chapter, I am excited that I will be revealing what I found.

For Your Consideration

Do you long to know true empowerment in your life? Do you

feel trapped in circumstances beyond your control? Are you suffering from feelings of frustration, despair or helplessness? These feelings are possibly the result of making choices that did not come from a place of power in your life or are the result of circumstances when you were still young and not in control.

Whatever the cause or the result, true empowerment is the birthright of everyone. And it can be yours too! The fact is, no one can give it to us. We have to grasp it for ourselves. We can be in control of our lives and our feelings. It is a choice we can make, but herein lies a problem. Most people find making that choice next to impossible. Dreaming of finding your real treasure can be simply that: a dream that never gets fulfilled. You can quickly feel overwhelmed by fear and rising anxiety at even the thought of making a start.

The good news is that following *The Secret of The Alchemist*, as revealed in this book, is a proven path to success that has been walked by a multitude before you. As you read this book, you will find all the insights you need to turn your dreams into reality and live a truly fulfilled life. All you need is to really want it!

Chapter 2

The Secret of The Alchemist Revealed

In the introduction to this book, I recalled how in the time following my encounter with Paulo Coelho, I was driven by the overwhelming desire to discover the secret that I believed lay hidden in *The Alchemist*. I wanted to gain full benefit from the power that Paulo had promised. I was convinced the answer lay in his story, and I wanted to discover the insights to find the full treasure on offer.

The answer was surely more than simply following your dreams, I thought. So I made a start by dissecting each character and event in the story to see if there was something hidden in there I could uncover. If you have read *The Alchemist*, you will recognize them.

I studied the significance of Melchizedek with his bejeweled breastplate, the crystal merchant and his unfulfilled dreams, the Englishman with his books, Fatima at the oasis, the camel driver with his folk wisdom and the thieves who beat Santiago almost to death before telling him where to find the treasure. Together they filled my imagination with colorful images, and I could see the parts they each played in Santiago's mission to find his treasure. But none of them revealed what I was looking for—the powerful life changing secret that had to be in there somewhere. I would have to try harder to find it.

Perhaps, I thought, one of the key secrets lay in the underlying psychological ingredients that have to do with the power of fable and mythology. Maybe Paulo had written a modern myth or fable that resonated in all of us as it drew upon universal, unconscious images we all share. Could it be that the story ignited deeply rooted symbolism beyond our conscious awareness? I decided I was onto something and should explore this more fully.

First I turned to the seminal work of Joseph Campbell, the late writer and teacher on comparative mythology and religion. In his book *The Hero with a Thousand Faces*, Campbell explains that time and again, in his studies of mythology from around the world, he uncovered common themes, plots and characters. Native American mythology, for instance, sometimes mirrors Ancient Greek myths, and themes from centuries-old Asian Indian stories appear in South American tribal traditions.

One of Campbell's most significant discoveries was a repetitive and collective theme that he called the "monomyth", popularly known as "The Hero's Journey" which features common distinctive elements: The hero must leave the ordinary world by accepting a call to adventure. At some point a mentor offers help to enable the hero to cross a guarded threshold into a supernatural world where trials and tests await. Ultimately this journey climaxes with a life threatening ordeal, which the hero survives with the help of allies. Just as the hero receives a reward, he decides to return to the ordinary world. But he faces more trials on the way home, where the reward can be used to improve the hero's life.

Campbell elaborated on these themes in his book *The Inner Reaches of Outer Space*. He writes that in The Hero's Journey, an unconscious primal power links all humankind, past and present, and even connects us to the cosmos and the forces within all life.

I applied Campbell's understanding of the power of myth to *The Alchemist*.

It seemed to me that *The Alchemist* did follow Campbell's well-worn mythical plotlines and drew on common themes of The Hero's Journey. The central plot of *The Alchemist* is a treasure hunt. Santiago the shepherd has a recurring dream under a sycamore tree growing in an abandoned church in the Andalusian countryside where he keeps his sheep. In the dream a child tells him if he leaves his home and travels overseas to Egypt, he will find hidden treasure buried near the pyramids.

Along the way he meets mentors and fellow travelers who encourage him on. When he finally arrives, he is attacked within inches of his life at the very moment he thinks he is about to discover the treasure. Yet one of his attackers takes pity on him and tells him of a similar dream he had when sleeping on the very spot where Santiago now lay blooded and close to death. The thief's dream was also about discovering treasure, only it was buried in a ruined church in Andalusia where shepherds and sheep slept. The treasure is indeed hidden beneath the roots of the sycamore tree, but the attacker, unlike Santiago, never pursued his dream. Santiago recovers from the attack, makes the journey back to the church and unearths a chest of Spanish gold coins.

There was no question in my mind that *The Alchemist* qualifies as a unique and powerful version of The Hero's Journey. I also discovered that the story draws on older myths from Indian, Persian and Arabian folklore that date back at least a thousand years. Its probable origin is an even older oral tradition, and it first appeared in English in the eighteenth century as one of the stories in a version of *The Arabian Nights* — the characters and plot are different, but the theme is identical and the moral universal.

What is this fable trying to tell us? Is it that we already possess the treasure of wisdom and its power to transform our lives for the better, but we have to embark on a conscious journey of discovery to unearth it? Yes, I believe that is exactly the message, and that journey is both inward and outward. The inner journey entails spending time listening to our heart and learning what is true and what is not. The outward journey is a manifestation of the inward one and is experienced through our thoughts, words, choices and actions. The lesson of the fable is easy to understand: our greatest treasure already lies within us, and it is ours to discover if we are prepared to take the inward journey to find it.

The story and its moral certainly resonate with anyone who

has embarked on the road to true empowerment, and I was hoping this would explain to me why that would make *The Alchemist* a bestseller. Sadly, it did not. I knew I was getting closer, but I wasn't there yet. Keep digging, I told myself.

I decided to go back to the very start of *The Alchemist*, where Santiago's journey to discover the treasure begins with a dream. Could it be that the secret is the dreamlike quality of the story? Santiago tells an old Gypsy woman he has twice dreamed about a child appearing while he was in a field with his sheep. The child is playing with the sheep when she suddenly takes him to the Egyptian pyramids and explains that this is where he will find his treasure. But both times, just as he is about to discover the exact location, he wakes up.

There are probably more books written about the significance of dreams and their place in the human psyche than almost any other topic associated with psychology. From Greek mythology to Sigmund Freud, dreams are seen to convey either coded messages from the gods or symbolic meanings from our unconscious. We are told they deliver important information we need to pay attention to in our waking lives and that consequently anyone who can help interpret them has a valuable gift. For the first time in my study of the book, I felt I was very close to unveiling the secret. Perhaps it lives in Santiago's dream?

Santiago believed there was a message in his dream, and so he approached the Gypsy, albeit with mixed satisfaction at the result. Surprisingly, she tells him to take the dream literally. He should go to Egypt in search of the treasure. There is no doubt that he was expecting something more profound. He had asked for an interpretation of a dream, only to be told he already had the answer. "Do what the dream says," she told him, "and you'll become a rich man." But I also remember thinking, when I first read that passage, that if Sigmund Freud had analyzed Santiago's dream, he probably would have agreed he had an unconscious desire to get rich. Yet somehow, I did not think this was simply a rags to riches story.

What I did now believe was there is a much deeper and life changing message hidden in that dream. I reread it a dozen times and eventually discovered I was right.

The significance is there right at the beginning of the story; but if I had blinked when reading it, I might have missed it.

The child in Santiago's dream is a girl.

She is mentioned only fleetingly but, to my mind, she is possibly one of the most significant characters in the story. In my search for age-old themes, I may have found the most important one. If one of the answers to *The Secret of The Alchemist* is the girl in the dream, then I've hit the jackpot!

Students of William Shakespeare will share my excitement because the girl child in the dream is very similar to something they've read before. In his play, *The Winter's Tale,* Shakespeare writes of a shepherd, a female child, a dream, a tree and the surprise discovery of gold. I was very excited about finding this connection, because to me it meant I may have stumbled upon a significantly important mythological theme.

In the plot of *The Winter's Tale,* one of the heroines is born in a prison where her father, Leontes, King of Sicilia, has sent her mother, Hermione because he wrongly believes she has been unfaithful to him. Leontes sends Antigonus to take the baby and leave her on the seacoast near a desert. In a dream, Hermione, who is now dead, appears to Antigonus and tells him to name her child Perdita, which means "the lost one" in Italian. Antigonus takes pity on Perdita and keeps her in a safe place near the desert, but he is chased away and eaten by a bear. Luckily, a shepherd living nearby comes to see what the noise is all about. He finds Perdita under a tree, along with a cloth sack full of gold, which Antigonus left with the child. The shepherd adopts Perdita, yet eventually, in her teenage years, her true royal heritage is discovered and she lives happily ever after with a handsome prince.

I reflected again on the girl child in Santiago's dream and how she's calling to him to find the treasure. The parallels are clear: he's a shepherd, and he's sleeping under a tree. Eventually, by listening to the girl child, the shepherd finds the gold on that very spot. What I see here now, too, is an example of Joseph Campbell's theory of the universal meanings within mythology. *The Winter's Tale* and *The Alchemist* both resonate within us because they are symbolic of a deeper truth. So what is this truth, and the hidden secret I was searching for?

In Perdita's tale, she possesses the gold that makes the benevolent shepherd rich because he cares for her and comes to appreciate the value of her heritage. In the story of Santiago, he listens to the girl in the dream and discovers the location of his treasure on the very spot where he had the dream.

What is the significance of this similarity of symbols in the two stories? I decided its import is, we ignore at our peril the voice of the inner feminine within our soul. She really does know where we will find our treasure.

It was Carl Jung who attributed a feminine persona "the anima" to these positive qualities in men and an equivalent masculine persona: "animus" in women. For anyone interested in this fascinating study of anima, animus, and archetypes, it is worth further reading of Jung's *Collected Works*. But here I want to simply focus on their significance in Santiago's unconscious.

Had I discovered, wrapped up in Jung's archetypal theories, *The Secret of The Alchemist?* Does the internal feminine archetype in men and the counterpart masculine archetype in women hold the key to finding true empowerment? Certainly, the story of *The Alchemist* may be about a boy on a journey to find his treasure, but the start of that journey begins with him getting in tune with his inner feminine side. She temptingly fills his mind with hope and a dream he cannot ignore. It could be a waste of his time, and he is free to ignore the dream; but then again, what if she is right? There may be untold treasure to be unearthed.

I pondered further. Is that the role of the girl in the dream here? Does she represent the part of our soul that challenges the pragmatic masculine within men and women? When we listen to our inner feminine, have we discovered the powerful element that has made Paulo's book a mega bestseller?

Deep down I had an unsettling feeling that this was not the case. So then, what to do? Would I have to start over again in my search for the secret of *The Alchemist's* incredible success?

It was around the time I was pondering the direction of my research when I received an unexpected call in my office in Sydney. I was taken totally by surprise by who was calling me.

"Is that Colm? This is Wayne Dyer."

Dr. Wayne Dyer was one of our publishing house's celebrity authors and a leading motivational speaker. We had just published his new book, *Real Magic,* and it looked all set to be another bestseller. He was calling me from his home in the USA.

"Hi, Wayne, yes, this is Colm." I was slightly awestruck at receiving a direct call from him. "How nice to speak to you. How can I help?"

"Colm, I hear you're something of an alchemist and performed some real magic with Paulo's book."

I paused as I considered that Wayne must have heard about the initial success of *The Alchemist* in Australia.

"Thanks for the compliment," I said, "but I wouldn't call it magic. I simply made the decision on how many copies we'd print, and it seems I even underestimated that."

"Well I *would* call it magic." Quickly Wayne got to his point. "Let's make sure you do the same with my book. I'm very widely known in Australia, and I want you to make your magic happen for my book too. Thanks in advance, and have a great day!" Then he hung up.

I was flattered to have received a call from such a famous and respected inspirational teacher and writer like Dr. Wayne Dyer. His challenge to me was clear, and it filled me with some anxiety that I might not be able to deliver to the level of his expectations.

I happened to have a copy of *The Alchemist* on my desk at the time, and as I put the phone down, I looked at its cover and reflected on what Wayne had just said. I continued staring at the cover of Paulo's book for several minutes as the title stared back at me.

And then, at that moment, a feeling of overwhelming elation swept over me. Finally, I realized what the ultimate secret was! The reason the book had been such a success was suddenly obvious. It had been there all the time, just like all the best kept secrets, in plain sight for all the world to see.

The ultimate secret of *The Alchemist* is the power of alchemy!

How could I have missed it all this time? *The Alchemist* is not just a gripping fable about a boy following his dreams. It's more than another version of The Hero's Journey or getting in touch with our inner feminine. The story is about how all of us can tap into the power of ancient alchemy to create magic and change lives!

My mind raced. Was this really why Paulo's book had been so successful? Was he telling us that if we want true empowerment in our life then we need to embrace the ancient art of alchemy?

My next question was possibly even more critical.

Did Paulo use alchemy to help him become a successful writer? Was *The Alchemist* written using alchemical principles?

In the terminology of Wayne Dyer, is *The Alchemist* a magic book?

The answers to those thoughts came thick and fast. The book certainly engages the reader for unfathomable reasons other than those I could immediately identify. Over time, it has remained popular for new generations, as readers still recommend it to one another. Could its extraordinary appeal be based on some mystical influence far beyond and perhaps deeper than the story itself?

My rational, logical mind instantly wanted evidence for this outlandish "alchemy magic" theory. So I decided to look beyond the book and examine how Paulo came to write the book in the first place.

Almost instantly I recalled Paulo telling me *The Alchemist* only took two weeks to write because, "The book was already written in my soul."

That led me to think that maybe Paulo used the principles of ancient alchemy to draw upon his unconscious for inspiration. This was a compelling thought but not really evidence of a "magic" origin of the story.

I then considered that the book was not an instant success, yet later became a phenomenon. It was originally published in Portuguese in 1988, by a small Brazilian publishing house, which cautiously only printed 900 copies and then let it go out of print.

But then I recalled Paulo telling me that he and his wife spent a forty-day vacation in the Mojave Desert south of Las Vegas. He did not relate what he experienced there, except he did say he "went off" into the desert alone every day.

What actually happened in that desert? Thinking about this, I now had my suspicion, based on his comments to me at our dinner, that he may have somehow used the techniques of ancient alchemy to bring something he really wanted into being.

I also recalled Paulo saying that, upon returning from the solitude of the desert, he had been more convinced than ever that he had written a great book. He then offered it to a major Brazilian publisher, which, according to Paulo, "for reasons the publisher could not explain," felt compelled to publish the book again in Portuguese. This time, "miraculously," Paulo said, it sold half a million copies. In Brazil, that's a bestseller! I now began to think this did not happen by chance. Paulo had made it happen by some supernatural force!

What happened next with *The Alchemist* was another out-of-the-ordinary publishing feat. The world rights were offered, and snapped up by HarperCollins, a major global publisher in the USA. Soon after, the first English-language manuscript ended up on my desk in Australia. As we already know, I was instantly convinced this was a bestseller; and it was. Was this just a coincidence or was I the right person, in the right place, at the right time to bring it to my colleagues' attention around the world?

Then I remembered Paulo's book *The Pilgrimage*, published just before *The Alchemist*, which was a fictionalized story of his "magical" experiences on the pilgrim's road to Santiago de Compostela and how in that story he was initiated into the fictional Master of the Order of the RAM – a symbolic invention to help with the drama in his story.

On rereading *The Pilgrimage*, it became clearer to me that most of the events in the story were purely fictional and that the book was a cloak of symbolism for something much more important. Behind the imagery, I now suspected, he was hiding his experience of using the power of ancient alchemy. Furthermore, the link between *The Pilgrimage* and his very next book, *The Alchemist*, is his use of the name Santiago. This was not a coincidence.

Finally, when I reflected on my own experience with Paulo at that evening in Sydney, it sealed my belief in my theory. Paulo had specifically told me he had spent a whole day calling on the universe on my behalf, and so enabled me to achieve whatever I wanted. It occurred to me I had never really pondered what he must have done at a practical level for a whole day for me. What did he do to make this happen? I finally realized that the answer, as with so many of my questions, lay within *The Alchemist* itself.

I was now convinced. *The Alchemist* is Paulo's instructions on how to apply the insights of ancient alchemy, and he used this knowledge to work his miracle for me. The power of ancient alchemy is the ultimate secret of *The Alchemist*.

The choice of the title of *The Alchemist* is not an allegory for anything else. How had I missed this even from the first time

I picked up the manuscript? The story is about how Santiago meets the alchemist, who helps him, too, become an alchemist. *The Alchemist* is a guide on how to perform real miracles in your life using ancient alchemy.

"Thanks, Wayne Dyer!" I said aloud. "I finally get it! There is such a thing as real magic, and how to create magic is there for all to find in *The Alchemist.*"

The truth of *The Alchemist*, finally openly revealed, is that we, too, can become real alchemists in our world today by following the alchemical process. I now understood why the story has been so amazingly popular. It was created out of alchemy and has a miraculous quality that has drawn millions of readers into its world. It has influenced so many lives because it really does contain the formula we need to transform our lives and the world around us for the better; even if we fail to recognize it when we read the story. This is the ultimate secret to finding our treasure, our destiny and true empowerment.

This, I now believe, was Paulo's gift to me: I would discover the ability to create miracles through an understanding of alchemy and share this gift with anyone who wants the same power in their life.

For Your Consideration

It may be that you already guessed that the ultimate secret is all about transformation through following the process outlined in ancient alchemy—and that this is the reason you are reading this book. If so, I hope not to disappoint you as I outline the powerful insights I have gained on this subject, and will reveal in the following chapters.

On the other hand, if the concept of exploring alchemy itself, which might seem to you an outmoded or even strange topic, leads you to question whether any of this is worthy of your time, then I can understand how you feel. I initially had exactly the same reaction. My hope is that your curiosity has been sufficiently piqued, and that you want to read on.

If either of the above applies to you, I can guarantee one thing for certain. Any understanding you will gain of the alchemical process of transformation as outlined in *The Secret of the Alchemist* will be of lifelong benefit to you and everyone in your world.

Also, as you reflect on the insights I have discovered, I repeat my promise that Love will lead you forward to give you everything you need to transform your life toward a place where you will see miracles happen.

Chapter 3

Alchemy – A Brief Introduction

Welcome to the world of alchemy.

When I discovered *The Alchemist* was all about alchemy, I knew absolutely nothing about its beliefs, history or key figures, even though I had been a high school history teacher. My knowledge was limited to what I had read in *The Alchemist* and that gave only a sketchy outline. For that reason, I decided to dive into researching the topic from scratch. What I uncovered was much more than an esoteric cult that believed lead could be turned into gold. What I found changed the course of my life forever.

In this chapter I want to bring not only some knowledge but also context to our understanding of ancient alchemy, along with my insights on how this knowledge helped me unearth the valuable secret to empower our lives today.

Ancient alchemy has a long, misunderstood and maligned history. The anti-alchemy lobby has been so successful through the centuries that for me alchemy meant little more than an occult form of wizardry that I vaguely thought was banned. At best, I regarded an alchemist as a near-mythological figure of the past who was stereotyped as typically male, slightly mad and crazily obsessed by the greed for gold.

Although in my bibliography I suggest some good books on this esoteric subject, I have no desire to turn this book into a history of alchemy. Yet as background to my major theme, I do want to introduce the perspective that alchemy was a major force that shaped culture and thought in the ancient world and still in some ways influences how we see the world today. I would even go as far as to say that in my view the ancient alchemists possessed a wisdom that is unknown to most people but has helped progress humankind.

As I began my informal study of alchemists, what I wanted to know at first was simply who these people were, where they came from and why they thought they could turn lead into gold. Their mythological origin goes back thousands of years to ancient Egypt, then rose to immense influence during the Greek and Roman empires and disappeared after the Middle Ages—a victim of the age of science and reason, as well as the end of the dream of turning lead into gold. Yet sadly, the valuable wisdom at alchemy's center was buried along with it.

But perhaps the ancient alchemists helped to hasten its demise by hiding what they believed mostly in secrecy behind closed doors, by deliberately cloaking their discoveries in undecipherable code and symbols and by losing their credibility to charlatans and fraudsters who masqueraded as the real thing but degraded their work.

Thanks to modern fantasy fiction, I was familiar with the idea that alchemists worked in their secret laboratories to try to create The Philosopher's Stone. At one time it was said that even a sliver of the mythical stone could turn lead into gold, and the alchemist would become rich forever. But as I continued to read up on the subject, I discovered that much of alchemy carried a deeper symbolism. To my surprise, I found, hidden behind the ancient alchemists' cloud of mystery and strange symbols, a blueprint for how to live a life of true empowerment. The person we need to thank for helping to uncover this hidden wisdom of the ancient alchemists is none other than the late Carl Jung.

It seems that, buried beneath the ancient alchemists' symbolism, Jung discovered a direct correlation of thinking that aligned with his theory of analytical psychology, and in particular the development of his psychology of the unconscious. (See his *Psychology and Alchemy*, in Volume 12 of the *Collected Works of C.G. Jung*). He found that connection so significant that he devoted the last thirty years of his life to studying and practicing the art of alchemy.

For me, discovering Jung's devotion to alchemy was a major eureka moment. I knew enough of his theory of analytical psychology to quickly see how he had made the connection. It is important to our insights concerning true empowerment to understand how Jung linked alchemy and the psychology of the unconscious.

Jung states that our thoughts and behavior are driven at two levels of the mind, the conscious and the unconscious. We are aware of our conscious mind; this is where our thoughts exist moment by moment. In our unconscious mind, automatic processes drive us along through life by way of instinct, suppressed memories and underlying motivations of which we are not necessarily aware. (See Jung's *The Structure and Dynamics of the Psyche.*)

In his theory of the unconscious, Jung agreed with Sigmund Freud, the father of psychoanalysis, that our personality is rooted, mostly without our knowledge, in our unconscious. For example, if we have a naturally jovial disposition, that trait comes from our unconscious. We feel happy most of the time and, even when our circumstances are grim, we are generally able to see the bright side. At the other extreme, we may be permanently melancholy, despite there being no direct or situational reason to feel unhappy. Both personality characteristics spring from the unconscious, without any deliberate effort or conscious thought on our part.

Then Jung goes one step further, suggesting that within the unconscious is another, even deeper level. At this depth there exists an accumulation of inherited unconscious thought processes that he called "archetypes," made up of experiences, figures and images. These exist in the unconscious of all of us, simply because we are human.

In his theory of archetypes, he refers to in-built themes and images which contain material from our entire species that has been passed down as we have evolved. These images have universal meanings and create the symbolic structure by which we understand the world and our place within it. For example, he says these can be discovered primarily through story, art, religions or dreams. In a nutshell, Jung holds that we behave and have images of behavior based on preset patterns or an order that is already programmed into our minds. The Hero's Journey we looked at in the last chapter is a great example of this.

For instance, someone who has just performed a heroic act to save someone's life will often say, "I'm not a hero, I just did what needed to be done. I didn't even think about it." That is the manifestation of the hero archetype.

Or when characters in a film are faced with a devil from the dark side who tempts them to stray from their good deeds, the devil figure is an archetypal persona in action. The point is that neither the hero who saves a life nor the author who pens the story of the devil is necessarily conscious of what they have expressed; but we all recognize the manifestation and can identify with it.

I like to think of an archetype as a monarch's head imprinted on a coin; it is a reminder of who is in charge. In this case we are the subjects of a ruling set of principles indelibly imprinted in our nature and to which we owe unquestioning allegiance. Or, to put it another way, it is the currency of our unconscious minds that we trade between us as a species.

Jung also postulated that archetypes are not merely human psychic phenomena but also form the bridge from the human mind to all physical matter. This assertion may be stretching our credibility tolerance levels as citizens of the era of technology, but I want to explore this theory because I genuinely believe it holds another vital insight into the importance of alchemy.

In other words, if Jung is correct, we are joined in a tangible way to everything, seen and unseen, by the very fact of our existence; and alchemy is the key to unlocking that connection.

Further, Jung writes in *Symbols of Transformation* that the ancient alchemists believed they must inwardly become the change they hoped to create. They called this process of turning lead into gold "transmutation" the reflection of the inner process of transformation.

Jung concluded that wholeness, or what he termed "individuation", was the final result of the process of transformation. This was the secret work that the ancient alchemists were engaged in, even though it was not until Jung came along that we would be able to describe what they did in modern terms we can understand. Successfully integrating our conscious and unconscious is the road to true empowerment, and most of this book is devoted to my experience in attempting to follow that road.

People who have reached Jung's level of individuation are those who bring about positive change in their world. They are typically people who have a realistic view of life and themselves, including the ability to laugh at their own flaws. They act with personal integrity without losing the ability to see things through childlike eyes. They love deeply and are capable of forgiveness and unconditional love.

This is the most important point of the alchemical process of transformation, as I have discovered, and it is why the ancient alchemists spent their lives devoted to it. If, as Jung believed, we are in fact connected in every way, both psychically and physically, to everything in the cosmos, then the person who is pursuing true empowerment can affect the outcome of the course of their lives and the world around them. This is the power of alchemy. They can turn the ordinary into gold!

* * *

At the beginning of *The Alchemist*, Santiago is a young soul still in the early stages of finding his way through life. He has already made some progress towards finding self-determination along the lines of Jung's process of individuation. We learn that he decided not to become a priest, as his parents had wanted. He was well-educated and had an enquiring mind; two key ingredients that he thought he needed to make his own way in life. Because he loved to travel, he became a shepherd so he could discover the world for himself. The scene is set for the analogy of alchemy to play out.

If the story follows the alchemical process as understood by Jung (and I believe it does), then some of the insights I describe in this chapter should be present in the plot. I will illustrate how these insights are indeed embedded into every level of secret I discovered in *The Alchemist* and how we can draw on their significance to our own benefit.

To recap, as the story begins, Santiago is so disturbed by his recurring dream that he fears he might be missing out on more in life than is currently his lot. He has listened to the girl child in the dream, and she has inspired him to reach out to someone he thinks may know the answer.

As we have seen, dreams and dreamlike states are the key realm of connection between the conscious and the unconscious; dreams are where the unconscious is joined to what in *The Alchemist* is called the "soul of the world" or in Jungian terms the collective unconscious.

In alchemy it is essential to pay attention to the images, characters and events of our unconscious dreams, as well as our conscious aspirations and ambitions—much as Jung did when formulating his theory of analytical psychology.

With that background in mind, we return to the beginning of the story of Santiago. He wants to know what his dream means. He goes to the Gypsy woman because he has heard she can interpret dreams. She tells him that to find the treasure he must take his dream literally and go to Egypt and visit the pyramids.

To me, this is a clear indication that *The Alchemist* is all about following the alchemical process. The metaphor of Santiago's dream is just that, if he wants to discover his treasure he must follow the ways of alchemy, which originated in Egypt where, not coincidentally, the pyramids still stand. Once we know this to be a fact in the story, the message of the dream becomes simple. Our treasure can be found by following the alchemical process.

We know the goal of the ancient alchemists was always ultimately to discover the highest levels of wellbeing, materially and spiritually. In Santiago's dream this is summarized by treasure. As we read the story, we see how on his journey to discover his treasure, Santiago passes through various stages of transformation of his own soul to reach the point of true empowerment, to unearth his treasure. These, as we shall see further on in this book, are the two inseparable parts of alchemy.

However, Santiago does not want to hear about going to Egypt to find his treasure at the pyramids. He decides never again to believe in his dreams. It is unclear in the story whether Santiago is reluctant to follow the process of transformation because, like all of us by nature, he wants to avoid the hard work that would entail, or because he thinks there must be an easier way to get rich without having to leave what he knows and where he feels safe. Either way, Santiago's initial reaction to the dream is one of ignoring the message.

In the story it is no coincidence that the treasure is buried in a church that has been abandoned. The roof has collapsed and a sycamore tree is growing up through the ruins. This aptly describes the lowly value most of us place on our dreams and by implication our unconscious. It is as if we have abandoned our souls. We no longer respect the inner voice of our hearts and instead fill our lives with empty distractions that pass the time but never take us forward. The net result is often a feeling of dissatisfaction and a loss of any meaning to life.

Yet our souls are the home of our dreams and the root of

our real desires, although often these dreams and desires are so deeply buried that we no longer are even aware of them. Are we like Santiago? Are we made uneasy by the fact that we may be missing out on the true purpose for our lives? Is this why we love the story of *The Alchemist* and want to know its secret?

It is a truism that any transformation towards true empowerment must begin with self-awareness and a deliberate self-determination to change. Without those attributes, we are in danger of stumbling through life in a fog, not knowing how it will unfold; our days are left to chance, and each begins with a roll of the dice where we have no control over what will turn up. We are merely the victims of circumstance.

Or even worse, we may believe our life is dictated by some sort of predetermined destiny and we have no say in the outcome— so why bother thinking about trying to change things? In this instance we take on the role of being victims of fate.

The Alchemist is very clear on this. The notion that we have no control over the course of our lives—that we're merely the victims of fate—is by far the most damaging and destructive belief we can hold. If that supposition were true, then it is indeed the cruelest joke to be played on us all: a deity who has total control of an individual's destiny, with the power to wreak good and evil at whim, is robbing the person of all true empowerment. Unfortunately, this definition of destiny sits within multiple faith traditions as well as in cultural superstitions and folklore.

The story of *The Alchemist* suggests an alternative viewpoint: we can create our own destiny. We are not passive passengers on the ship of life to be taken wherever the wind blows without any determination over the destination. We can seize the wheel and steer it to where we want to go. We can become the masters of our fate, the captains of our soul! The outcome may not always be what we initially had hoped for but at least it will be the result of our plans and our choices.

For Your Consideration

So how do you know when you are following your true destiny?

You know you are on the right path when you make a conscious decision to pursue your dreams and your life is full of enthusiasm and purpose. You will experience a sense of awe, wonder and potential about the events in your daily existence. You know there is a loving purpose and design to your life, and you are free to choose the direction to travel. You are "following your bliss", as Joseph Campbell describes it, and your life is full of magic and abundance.

"If only it were that easy," I hear you say, and you are right. It's not easy at all! If it were, then everyone would be doing it, and clearly they are not. But if you really want to join those who have discovered the steeper but more rewarding path through life, then it's never too late to commit to transformation. I can guarantee that it won't be a walk in the park. But I can also say from my own hard work that it is the only way to truly live a life full of joy! This is because as we commit to this path, we will find the power and strength to overcome the inner and outer obstacles that want to rob us of a joyous existence.

Let me be clear on this: the alchemical process of transformation to true empowerment can only take place when you fully determine to take control of your choices and follow your heart. If that is the choice you have made, then your treasure awaits you. What's more, all the power of Love is with you as you make that commitment, the Love that fully embraces all that you are and will become. As you read this book, I have asked Love to give you everything you need to find the greatest joy in life and the power to change your world for the better; that is, if you truly want it!

Chapter 4

Enter Melchizedek

When I reread *The Alchemist* with a fuller understanding of alchemy and its true purpose in mind, I was finally convinced that the fable is so much more than a good read about a boy chasing his dreams; it encapsulates some of the deepest alchemical truths about how we can influence or even change the outcome of our life and our world for the better. Very early on in the story, too, I discovered the mysterious and influential character called Melchizedek and decided he represented the next essential step in the alchemical process of transformation to find our true inner self.

It will help us understand the part this character plays if I share some of the background about who Melchizedek is in the context of myth and historic alchemy.

Reportedly, we find the source of alchemy five thousand years ago in Egyptian mythology in the story of the powerful god Thoth, who was the go-between of the worlds of matter and the spirit. The ancients believed alchemy was literally a gift from the gods and it was first practiced near where the Great Pyramids still stand. Ancient alchemists revered Thoth as the creator of transformation in nature and humans and believed he recorded his teaching on the "Emerald Tablet." (More about the Emerald Tablet later, and in general more about this subject in Geraldine Pinch's book on *Egyptian Mythology*.)

Thoth is generally considered the father of all alchemy, and alchemists believe he has appeared time and again in significant moments of history. Moreover, they cast Thoth as the one who put various life purposes in the hearts and souls of humans, such as the ambition to get rich, to be healthy, to care about the welfare of society and to live in peaceful communion with the universe.

But what brings this ancient lore within the Judeo-Christian tradition is the belief of European alchemists that Moses— remember, he led the Jews from captivity in Egypt to the Promised Land—was schooled in the Egyptian myths, including the legend of Thoth. There are so many parallels and similarities between early Egyptian myths and Jewish mythology written by Moses, especially regarding the beginning of creation, that it should perhaps be no surprise that Thoth—this time under the name Melchizedek—makes an appearance in the story of Abraham. (For much more on this see P.G. Maxwell-Stuart's *The Chemical Choir*, which is a good history on alchemy.)

We find him in the Old Testament of the Bible:

"And Melchizedek king of Salem brought forth bread and wine: and he was the priest of the most high God. And he blessed him, and said, Blessed be Abram of the most high God, possessor of heaven and earth: And blessed be the most high God, which hath delivered thine enemies into thy hand. And he gave him tithes of all."
(Gen. 1.14.)

The implication is clear. Alchemy not only exists in ancient Egyptian tradition but also in Jewish tradition, and therefore by default in Christian tradition. Melchizedek, like Thoth, is still timeless and from everywhere; he is able to reveal secrets; he can open the eyes of our understanding and most significantly he is the go-between God of the Bible and man. This priestly purpose of Melchizedek as an intermediary is continued in Jewish tradition in the role of the High Priest of the Old Testament.

* * *

Likewise, Melchizedek makes an appearance in the story of *The Alchemist*.

We find him in the most public and everyday place, just at the point when Santiago has decided to ignore his dream. Instead, he intends to travel with his sheep to a village where he hopes to see a girl he met the previous year on his travels. He is a few days away from his destination, when he rests in a village plaza to read a book he has just bought. Suddenly, an old man named Melchizedek appears as if from nowhere and without any formal introduction he engages in conversation with Santiago.

Melchizedek's initial questions and Santiago's reactions are interesting. Even as Santiago continues reading his book, Melchizedek points to the people in the plaza and asks the young shepherd to tell him what they are doing. Then he asks for some wine and wants to see what Santiago is reading. Even as Santiago considers simply getting up and moving away, he obliges Melchizedek out of a sense of respect for an older person. He gives Melchizedek the book partly in the hope that the old man cannot read and will be embarrassed into leaving him alone.

At that moment Melchizedek reveals his identity. He is from many places but was born in the ancient Middle Eastern town of Salem, where he is the king. His name is Melchizedek and he likens himself to a "Warrior of Light."

This is clearly a reference to the character of Melchizedek as he appears in Jewish scriptures.

Melchizedek knows all about the book Santiago is reading. He also knows Santiago's dream and offers to tell him how to find the treasure in exchange for one-tenth of his sheep. He proceeds to write something mysterious in the sand where they are sitting. Then something quite supernatural takes place.

Melchizedek opens his cape. A brilliant light reflects from his chest and blinds Santiago for a few moments. When he can see again, he is able to read what Melchizedek has written in the sand: the names of Santiago's family and secret things that he has never told anyone.

A few scenes later we discover that the bright light came from an unusual source. In continuing to liken this story of Melchizedek to that of a Judaic priest of the Old Testament, both of them wear a gem-studded breastplate:

"And Aaron shall bear the names of the children of Israel in the breastplate of judgment upon his heart, when he goeth in unto the holy place, for a memorial before the Lord continually."
(Ex. 28.29)

Biblical scholars agree the breastplate represents the God of Israel's salvation of the people of Israel and deliverance from their enemies and is worn by the High Priest when he enters the presence of the Almighty within the Holy of Holies, the inner sanctuary of the Tabernacle. The High Priest would enter once a year on the Day of Atonement, or Yom Kippur, wearing the breastplate to remind the God of Israel of his saving grace towards the people of Israel. This was the most sacred day in the Judaic calendar and the moment when the God of Israel and his people are reconciled through the sacrifice of a lamb with its blood taken into the sanctuary by the High Priest.

Much has been written about the Melchizedek in the Bible, both concerning his role in Christian teaching and his origins in Egyptian mythology. Jesus is even described in a New Testament epistle as being *"made a high priest forever after the order of Melchizedek."* (Heb. 6:20)

Perhaps we should step back a moment to fully digest the implications of what the story of *The Alchemist* is suggesting here. I believe this is a clear illustration of the ancient Egyptian alchemical tradition seeping into the roots of Jewish and Christian scriptures. What if alchemical truths were woven into the foundational beliefs of these two faith traditions, and at an orthodox level?

The Alchemist, I believe, is suggesting here that Santiago experienced a deepening of his Christian faith and a real encounter with Love through his meeting with Melchizedek. This, then, is one of our most significant insights into finding the treasure as well as a key understanding for anyone who wants to be transformed and create true gold in their world.

Certainly we can see that Santiago's moment of blindness is a pivotal event in his life story. The effect of the momentary blinding by the bright light from Melchizedek's breastplate is a life changing experience, and he instantly acquires a new level of awareness.

From this moment on, Santiago comprehends the world with new eyes. He is suddenly aware there is a power greater than himself at work in the world. This power knows everything about him, even his most private secrets. Melchizedek then explains not only who he is but also reveals Santiago's purpose in life and the benevolent intent of the "soul of the universe" to enable him to achieve it.

When Santiago asks why all this has been revealed to him, Melchizedek explains that he is clearly trying to discover his destiny. But now he knows that it is his responsibility, if not his obligation, to seek true empowerment and live life to the full. Melchizedek immediately tells him what he needs to do next. Santiago weighs his life options and chooses to follow his destiny.

He heads off for Egypt and the pyramids, where he will be exposed to the insights of alchemy, and at the end of the journey he will find gold.

The story of *The Alchemist* makes it clear that without an awakening of our souls or an opening of our eyes to the existence of Love, there is no way forward in the realization of our treasure. In the brief moment that was a window into eternity, when time stood still and he became blind, Santiago entered into a new relationship with Love. For him, Love was no longer something remote, distant or aloof. He was now aware that Love lived within his own being.

When Melchizedek comes to us, it's usually at a time we least expect and in a form we don't immediately recognize. If we were in any doubt about this, we find confirmation in Melchizedek's role in the story of Santiago, as an agent of Love in human form.

* * *

I was eighteen when Melchizedek sat down next to me and his name was Robert.

Robert lived in the room next to me in the university hall where I was a student in 1970. He was older than most of the rest of the students, and I certainly did not regard him as part of our group. This was the hippie era, when we were in the midst of a countercultural revolution. As far as we were concerned, Robert's dress, hairstyle and interests were old fashioned and not cool. So even though we all lived in close proximity, Robert remained something of an enigma to me. We would pass each other on campus with courteous greetings but in the space of a couple of months had never engaged in a genuine conversation. The point I'm making is the similarity of my experience to that of Santiago. Neither of us at this point in life particularly wanted to engage in conversation with a stranger.

Out of the blue one evening, Robert and I found ourselves alone in the common room kitchen of our university dorm. He smiled and asked how I was. I was busy making a snack and about to give a polite noncommittal reply when I sensed there was more than a passing curiosity in the tone of his voice.

I remember looking up and catching his gaze directed towards me, and I saw a genuine concern in his eyes. My instinct was to belittle the question by fobbing it off with some meaningless chatter about lectures and essays; but for some reason I did not. In that split second, I made the decision to give a real answer.

"To be honest, Robert, things aren't that great. In fact you could say they couldn't get much worse." I sensed he somehow already knew that, hence his question in the first place. I had no idea what he was going to say next.

He reached out to me with a small printed booklet and said, "I just thought you might find this useful. It really helped me when I was in a similar crisis. Maybe we should chat again in a week's time, when you've had a chance to read it and I can answer any questions you may have?"

"Thanks, Robert," I replied, not really sure how to respond to such a frank and simple offer as I stared at the booklet in my hand.

Robert smiled again and said, "You're welcome! I'll see you in week then?"

Somewhat confounded, I said, "Yes, okay." As he wished me a good evening, he turned and walked away without another word.

I was still staring at the booklet when I realized someone else might come into kitchen and keep me talking all evening. I grabbed my snack and returned to my dorm room. It was not until I closed the door, locking it behind me so I would not be disturbed, that I quickly realized this was a religious tract. My intellectual cynicism clicked in, ready to dismiss it out of hand. So this, I thought, is what Robert is peddling. He wants to convert me to his religion. I wasn't interested.

At that point in my life, I thought religion had caused more problems than good for the world.

As I briefly skimmed the booklet, I was not surprised to see the usual claims of some Christian groups about Christ's sacrifice to appease an angry God. To me, the very concept of a God who needed to punish the world he had created seemed medieval, and I was ready to throw the booklet into my trash can when I noticed a statement attributed to Jesus I had never read before:

"I am come that they might have life, and that they might have it more abundantly."
(John 10.10)

I must admit those words leapt out of the page and resonated with my own ruminations over the previous few months.

I was genuinely unhappy with the emotional quality of my life. Over the past few months I had become aware of how selfish I was. Even without discussing my feelings with anyone else, I could easily see how my inconsiderate and self-centered attitudes had led to toxic behavior toward those I loved most. Most importantly, I didn't feel in control of my life. I felt driven by uncontrolled emotional needs that were never satisfied, no matter how much I pandered to their demands. Deep within I longed to find a way to free myself from the power those needs had over me. I was definitely searching for a way to find true empowerment and take back control over my life. I understood abstractly the effects of hormones in adolescence, and I tried not to beat myself up about the powerful feelings that are normal at that age.

But classroom biology explaining the effects of normal teenage hormones was not providing a solution to the crisis I felt at that moment. I hoped for a better inner life, one that could be manifested in a fuller outer one: *"I am come that they might have life, and that they might have it more abundantly."* For me, this was definitely a timely message. It cut through all my intellectual cynicism about religion. It felt like a gift waiting for my acceptance.

Robert knocked on the door of my room exactly a week later, as he had promised. I invited him in and offered a seat.

"How," he began, "are things?"

"They've been better, thanks." I told him the booklet had raised more questions than answers about my emotional situation, and that the verse about abundant life had seemed to strike a chord.

Robert shared how opening his own life to discover Love had begun a process of emotional renewal which had led him to an ongoing sense of deep peace and direction.

As he was speaking, I felt myself letting go of my intellectual skepticism against anything that could not be identified as logical or scientific. Here was another human being who hardly knew me identifying with my emotional plight and making himself totally vulnerable. I felt that he completely understood my deepest fears and longings for a happier life.

No one had ever spoken to me of these things before, and in that moment of emotional truth and intimacy what he was saying instantly made perfect sense. But oddly, although I could hear Robert's voice, I was lost in my own thoughts until his next question broke into my trance-like state.

"Is there," he asked, "any reason why you can't open your life to Love right now?"

I remember answering that no, there was not, and then hearing him repeat that same scriptural quote of Jesus:

"I am come that they might have life, and that they might have it more abundantly." From somewhere deep within, a truth burst out of me. "I want that life!"

Robert then quoted aloud another verse:

"Behold, I stand at the door, and knock: if any man hear my voice, and open the door, I will come in to him, and will sup with him, and he with me."
(Rev. 3.20)

The last thing I remember saying, in what I understand now was the voice of what I have come to regard as my former life, was a prayer that Robert began and I repeated, in which I invited Love to transform my life with the abundance I wanted. I can't remember the exact words of this prayer, but I will never forget what came next.

Like Santiago, it was as if a blinding light made time stand still and Love flamed within the very depth of my being. What I experienced was as real as anything I have ever known before or since. For a moment of apparent transfiguration, Love was more real to me than life itself. I began to weep uncontrollably. The tears came from a place deep within, where for the first time I had a sense of being truly wanted and accepted for who I was.

I have no idea how long it was before Robert asked if I was okay. But I greeted him with a big smile and the understated answer, "The best I've ever felt!"

What I did not know at that point, was, I had experienced my first step toward transformation.

But for me, as it was for Santiago, I had no knowledge then of alchemy; and I would not be able to explain what had happened in those terms for another twenty-three years.

Yet I clung onto what I knew was true at the time: I had encountered Love, and it was unconditional. It was and is a Love that knew everything about me, and still loved me, even more than I loved myself. I also knew that my life and relationships would never be the same from that day onward, and that what I wanted more than anything else was that other people should be able to experience the Love I had found.

For Your Consideration

Are you searching for true empowerment? If your answer is "Yes," then you should know that this desire comes from Love. Even your aspirations for a better life come from this Love, and all you need to find your treasure is at hand. The first step is simply to ask for help and to know there are no conditions attached to receiving it:

"And I say unto you, ask, and it shall be given you; seek, and ye shall find; knock, and it shall be opened unto you. For every one

that asketh receiveth; and he that seeketh findeth; and to him that knocketh it shall be opened."
(Luke: 11.9-10).

No two encounters with Love are the same, and only you can judge if you have experienced it. No one religious system or faith tradition holds an exclusive right to Love. It will be your experience, in your way and in your time, without any pressure or coercion from Love.

True empowerment means no one can dictate how this will happen for you. It is a unique experience in which you will know you are loved unconditionally, for your own sake and not for what you can do or give in return. Love is no respecter of persons and is freely available to all. When you encounter the Love, a spark will be kindled in your heart, and this is the spark of light that initiates the process towards the creation of your Philosopher's Stone.

All intellectual understanding of human psychology, biology or physics is unable to substitute for the power of Love. It is Love that transforms because Love is the purpose of life.

You have that Love within you and around you and you can harness its power to transform your life.

In fact, the most important question to ask yourself at this moment is not, "Have I embraced Love?"

The most important question is, "Have I allowed Love to embrace me?"

If the answer is "No," then I recommend you do that now. Love will not let you down.

I repeat my promise: I have asked Love to give you everything you need to become the alchemist in your world, if you truly want it!

Chapter 5

Omens and Synchronicity

The process of transformation as followed by the ancient alchemists depends heavily on what we will call omens. The alchemists believed that if all is one, then it must be possible to receive and read messages from the cosmos to assist in their process and decision making. They believed that the elements of the cosmos participate in their choice to transform and create gold. If all things are connected, then we will see signs or omens to confirm our choice and direction when we are on the right path of our transformational process.

All ancient cultures, both Western and Eastern, incorporate omens somewhere within their folklore traditions because this is such a common—and, I would add, significant—phenomenon. Typically this ranges from highly complicated horoscopes to simple superstitions of good and bad luck. Somewhere within this potpourri of belief systems lies the phenomenon of coincidences as one of the most commonly recognized forms of meaningful omens.

Carl Jung in particular noticed how common coincidences occurred to his patients during psychoanalysis, so much so that he named the phenomenon "synchronicity" and wrote a famous book of that title.

In that book, he tells a story that seems to me to have direct relevance to *The Alchemist*. As Jung related in *Synchronicity*, one of his clients, who had been using her impressive intellect to dismiss her unconscious feelings and so resist his work with her, finally confessed to having a dream involving her receiving the gift of a golden beetle amulet. Such scarabs were common in Egyptian times and were worn to bring good fortune. But as she was relating her dream, Jung heard a gentle tapping at the window behind him and turned to see a large flying insect trying to enter his office. He opened the window, captured what turned out to be a similar beetle and presented it to her, saying, "Here's your golden scarab!" She immediately abandoned her resistance, and he was able to proceed to help her.

In his consideration of synchronicity, Jung did not go looking for meaning in every chanced happening. But he did identify that sometimes events took place in a moment of time that carried meaning for the observer but lacked any logical reason for their occurrence. Moreover, he observed that such events occurred more frequently with patients pursuing transformation and often seemed to speed the transformational process.

There are some interesting insights about synchronicity from Sir David Spiegelhalter, the contemporary British statistician whose work has influenced lifesaving medical research. He also has an ongoing fascination with coincidences in people's lives and looks for patterns that can be explained statistically on his website:

www.statslab.cam.ac.uk/Dept/People/Spiegelhalter/davids.html.

To date he has found no such patterns but suggests that the miracle here is that these recurrences have meaning to those who experience them—and for reasons other than any law of probability.

Perhaps that thought jibes with Jung's belief that synchronicity can be seen as a proof of the existence of a benevolent force at work within the cosmos that is directed towards the good of the human race. In his book *Synchronicity*, Jung concluded that science is no real help in explaining this and that it falls more within the ancient alchemists' understanding of the connectedness of all things to explain why they occur.

The ancient alchemists were in no doubt that when we pursue inner transformation with the intent of turning base objects into gold, we are following the true purpose of life. They were also certain that consequently all things will participate in the work and that the occurrence of omens will affirm this. Moreover, this assistance will be apparent at all stages of our alchemical transformation. The miracle will be that we see them and they will hold a meaning to encourage and direct us.

* * *

How will Santiago know when he is following the right path toward his treasure? Melchizedek says he will be directed through omens. All Santiago has to do is read them. Before he sets off on his journey, Melchizedek gives Santiago two stones taken from his breastplate. Urim and Thummim are the names of the stones, and their history is again linked to the Old Testament priests of the Bible who had embedded them in their breastplates.

When a decision or a choice of direction needed to be made, Urim was a black stone and stood for "Yes," and Thummim was white and signified "No." The stones symbolize that when Santiago is committed to finding his treasure, Love is with him and ready to guide and direct him through every moment of his life.

However, no sooner has Melchizedek given the stones to Santiago than he suggests there is a better way to know his true path through the desert. Instead of using the stones as some form of divination, he recommends the better way is to listen to his heart, or his intuition.

Santiago later discovers from the Englishman, another alchemist in the making, that the universal language of Love is indeed written in luck and coincidence. To illustrate that in a practical way, when Santiago meets the Englishman, he is introduced for the first time to the existence of alchemy and the alchemists. Santiago then learns that he possesses a natural intuition, which his mother used to call "hunches." This intuition allows him to immerse his soul into what is called the universal current of life, where everyone's journeys are connected and where he can know all he needs to know. He gives this a name:*"Maktub"*, meaning in Arabic, "It is written."

Omens as good luck and also coincidence appear in many ways for Santiago throughout the story. His friend buys his sheep and immediately he decides to go to Egypt. The stones Urim and Thummim fall through a hole in his pouch to stop him from abandoning his journey. Customers come to the crystal shop when he starts working there. The Englishman sees Santiago's stones and says they are an omen to show their paths are connected.

These coincidences encourage Santiago to believe he has chosen the right path to find his treasure even when events are difficult, painful and do not unfold as he would have hoped. Even so, there are times in the story when everything seems to be set against him and in fact his very life is in danger. But the story is full of Jung's synchronicity, and because it keeps Santiago moving in the right direction, we can see Love is being supportive. He discovers what many religious teachers call "grace." If we follow Jung's teachings, grace is manifested through what may seem like both positive and negative experiences.

My own life has been full of such meaningful experiences since I committed to transformation, to the point where following omens and recognizing luck has become a way of life. I could almost fill a whole book with the stories of where Love has aided and led me through omens, once I had the eyes to see them. To illustrate I want to give a very recent example.

My son was working on a new online movie streaming service he had created, and he needed a name for it. I volunteered to help, and we racked our brains for weeks to invent a name that would be memorable and was not already in use. We were really struggling and beginning to doubt if we would ever find one. In fact, the names I began to invent became so ridiculous that my son eventually banned me from submitting any more for his consideration. I do not give up easily, however, so I decided to quietly use the alchemical process to see if Love had a name we could use.

After several days of committing to the search for a name, I felt I had a clear direction to look for the names of the first cine projectors. I did find a list of names and gave my son one that I thought could work. His first reaction seemed quite positive, and he said he would do some more background research into the origins of the name.

To my surprise, he called me back the same day, excited with the news that the name I had chosen was the first cine projector used for public movie shows in North America and Canada and had been patented by Thomas Edison in 1874. I agreed that was a great pedigree and the name a perfect fit for his business.

Then he delivered the major surprise. The original Canadian distribution rights for the projector had been purchased by distant relatives of our family ancestors in Ireland who had migrated to Canada during the great famine. We were historically related and connected to the name I had chosen by using the alchemical process, and without my having any prior knowledge of that side of our family history. What I did know, however, was that this was an omen of the sort that Jung describes and a clear sign that my son should run with the name.

Jung would not have been shocked by my example. He would have said this was only another example of the meaningful coincidences that led to his theory of synchronicity. There is a universal principle at work here, but it not only applies to what may appear to be positive experiences. It can equally apply to negative experiences.

Sadly, in my early days of writing *The Secret of The Alchemist*, someone close to me died, and he had requested in his will that I should give the eulogy. But when I was asked by his family to help plan the funeral, it proved to be a challenge to find a day when the church and all the family were available. Several family members, including me, already had major commitments scheduled. I should add that I understand that grief and bereavement often trigger some unpredictable behavior; logic and reason can be overridden by emotions that may appear out of proportion.

It was in this context, after the family finally managed to find an appropriate date and we all gathered to console one another, that a problem occurred. A distant relative whom I rarely see blamed me for causing the family great distress by not being available on the date he had originally proposed, even though we had quickly all agreed on an alternative date.

When I gently tried to defuse his anger, which I realized must be rooted in his grief, he accused me of "having a way with words", and stormed off. He later returned and apologized for his outburst and we were reconciled. However, what he did not realize was, unwittingly his accusation of my "having a way with words" in fact had an opposite effect than what he had intended.

At the time I was engaged in a private struggle as to whether I had the literary skills to write something that others would find compelling. I received his outburst as an omen that I should keep writing this book, and I am grateful to him for the honesty of his feelings, even expressed in anger. The point being: not all omens appear in positive form initially, but they may direct us along the right path.

For Your Consideration

Have you been experiencing any remarkable coincidences or new omens since you began reading this book? If you want your life to transform toward true empowerment, then Love will begin to support you by giving you constant reassurances that you are on the right track.

You may find it useful to keep a note of each omen so you can recall them later if less than positive situations drive you to look for some encouragement. Now that you can see the omens in your life, you have the opportunity to ask your heart what a particular omen might mean.

For example, are you planning to move or travel for a specific purpose that you think will assist your transformation? In my experience, this is a classic situation where omens will appear to guide you as to go, if you have the eyes to see them.

I should add a word of caution. You will need to abandon the superstitions you have inherited and still carry with you. Omens are not related in any way to superstition. They have nothing to do with lucky charms, hexes or curses. This is not about seeing a black cat cross your path bringing bad luck or throwing salt over your shoulder if you spill it to avoid bad luck.

Superstition is another great lie that instills a sense of disempowerment. Superstitions are perpetuated by our upbringing as well as our cultural surroundings and habit; they should be discarded whenever you catch yourself repeating them. You should look to replace them with your own determination to follow the way of Love.

Love is trying to engage with you at every turn, and you can respond by committing to transformation and becoming aware of the omens.

Learning to see and understand the omens is like entering a new dimension of life. Welcome to this dimension of the world of alchemy. Remember, too, that I have asked Love to give you everything you need to become the alchemist in your world — and omens will be there to guide you.

Chapter 6

Into the Desert

As we have seen so far, transformation from base matter into pure matter is at the very heart of ancient alchemy. Moreover, alchemists believed the purification of base metals into gold and silver included the accompanying catharsis of the spirit from darkness to light.

The main question I was left with as a result of my research of the ancient alchemists was: how did they think this was possible?

The answer is wrapped up in their ultimate goal to create the Philosopher's Stone, which was made from what they called *"prima materia"*, Latin for "first matter". For the alchemists, prima materia was an invisible and yet bedrock component of everything that exists. What led to their iron-into-gold speculation, however, was their belief not only that all matter is alive but also that it can be transformed towards perfection if the prima materia—seen as a small spark of life buried within all matter—can be released within it. Jung, in *Psychology and Alchemy*, explains that the alchemists experimented for centuries on how to release that spark with heat, light or any one of limitless other possibilities.

We may never know whether the Philosopher's Stone was actually ever created in a physical sense. We do know, however, that over the centuries all this became more and more esoteric. Many alchemists came to believe that the Philosopher's Stone does exist in a dreamlike world between light and dark, energy and matter. But what perhaps was most intriguing about this whole search was the evolving belief that the Philosopher's Stone has the capacity to join all things together, heal divisions and unite opposites.

There were even two ways to achieve this: the more popular

but dangerous quick start "dry way" working with what alchemists called the "raging fires of our lower nature" or the "wet way" involving gradual initiation toward the state required to achieve personal transformation.

Santiago, in *The Alchemist*, of course was in a hurry to realize his dream and chose the way of the desert—the dry way—to achieve his transformation, and it is worth us looking now at what that will entail within the alchemical process.

In the alchemist's laboratory, the dry way begins with what was called the "black phase" in which matter is broken down into its constituent parts, followed by the "white phase" in which those base elements are purified. The final stage is the "red phase" in which the purified elements appear in the form of a reddish powder; this is the core ingredient of the Philosopher's Stone and could, alchemists believed, turn base metal into gold. The key point to remember here is the chemical process in the laboratory was a metaphor for the inner black, white and red phases the alchemist experienced.

Ancient alchemists refer to these three stages as the "*magnum opus*" or "great work". Significantly, the stages were later used by Carl Jung to identify the steps to psychological transformation, leading to the final result of true empowerment.

Both the alchemists and Jung considered the first black phase as the hardest and longest part of the great work. In the alchemist's laboratory it was often referred to as "mortification", which meant "facing the dead part", where the worthless and valueless properties of the physical matter ended up in a pile of ashes and the former characteristics could no longer be recognized. This process was often described by the alchemists as "facing the dragon".

The dragon, in the context of inner transformation, represents our dark side, the part of our nature that we would prefer to ignore or are in denial about. We fear the dragon and feel that if we face it, we will be consumed by it.

The dragon lives in our unconscious, and we mostly believe we have it firmly under control and can keep it hidden from public view. The dragon possesses all the fire and danger of the unwanted aspects of our humanity that we fear the most and the dragon is firmly in control of our lives.

Often we have become so detached from our true feelings and thoughts that we are completely unaware of ourselves whether we admit it or not. What the ancient alchemists—and later, Carl Jung—realized is, we have to face the dragon if we have any hope of achieving true wholeness and wellbeing.

Moreover, facing the dragon is the only path to true empowerment, because when we do find the courage to face it, we must draw from within the prima materia at the heart of all life to defeat it.

In particular the dragon symbolizes the elements of ourselves which live within what Jung called our "shadow". Robert Johnson, an esteemed Jungian analyst, wrote the definitive work on this subject, *Owning Your Own Shadow*. In it, he clearly outlines that psychological health and true empowerment can only be derived from the unity of our conscious and unconscious selves.

There is, however, some good news in this seemingly hopeless dilemma. The ancient alchemists had a clear understanding that our greatest treasure lies within this dark place, which is also home of the purest gold. As Jung wrote "...this means that the thing which we think the least of, that part of ourselves which we repress perhaps the most, or which we despise, is just the part which contains the mystery." (*The Red Book. Reflections on C.G. Jung's Liber Novus*, edited by Thomas Kirsch and George Hogensen.)

The alchemists understood that our weaker, least valued and unconscious self is not a mistake of nature. Our wounded self is not only represented by the base metal of the work in the alchemist's lab but also is indispensable for the accomplishment of the great work of producing the Philosopher's Stone.

Without the shadow part, there would be no way to make the alchemical gold.

If, however, we dare to embrace our shadow self and treat it with the respect and dignity it deserves—following the processes outlined in the black phase, all the power of Love will be there— despite our feelings to the contrary.

The alchemical black phase is all about breaking down and is not something we are going to enjoy; on the contrary it will feel as if we are descending into the pit of our own darkness, where the only light is from the metaphorical fire of hell. In the darkness we will feel alone and literally in the depths of despair.

This spiritual reduction process was portrayed as *The Dark Night of The Soul* in the famous poem by the 16th Century Catholic spiritual giant, St. John of the Cross. In essence, his point of view in this matter could be said to align with that of the ancient alchemists: if you want to transform to true empowerment, and deliberately follow the process of the black phase, the primary sensation will be a deep sense of meaninglessness.

This can be such a powerful and overwhelming experience that it is often compared to depression. It is a state where nothing seems to make sense anymore and everything is without purpose: our activities, our achievements, where we are going and what we considered important. Essentially the meaning we have given to our life collapses.

It is important to remember that these overwhelming feelings and sensations are real and not imagined. They are to be found in our unconscious and are dormant in all of us. We can either actively choose to face them using the alchemist's dry way or we can wait for them to break into our lives involuntarily over the course of our life, in the wet way. The alchemists believed the choice is ours. Santiago chose the dry way as he heads off into the metaphorical desert to find his treasure.

* * *

In the story of *The Alchemist*, Santiago meets again with Melchizedek, having committed to pursue his dream, and is given various gems of wisdom that he will need to see him through this hardest and longest stage of his journey. He has no idea what is about to happen, but he is prepared to accept the help on offer.

Melchizedek warns him of a "mysterious force" that he says appears to be negative but actually holds the secret to realizing his destiny. It will prepare his spirit and will reveal the "one truth" which is: when he really desires to change, that desire comes from the Soul of the Universe and is the purpose he is on earth to fulfill. Further, Santiago is told that the Soul of the Universe is nourished when people are happy and is equally influenced by people's unhappiness, envy and jealousy. He sums this up as: "all things are one."

Santiago then sets off across the sea to an unknown desert land, where the heat of the sun dries up everything. His journey toward his treasure will be a dry desert experience — the dry way of the ancient alchemists.

Not surprisingly, Santiago encounters an immediate setback when he arrives at the port in the land where his real journey will begin. Within one day he has lost everything he had taken with him by foolishly trusting a stranger with all the money he had collected to take him to the pyramids. He is in an unfamiliar land with strange ways, where they speak a language he does not understand, where he no longer has his identity as a shepherd and where he is penniless. These are all the expected feelings when entering the black phase using the dry way.

His immediate reaction is self-pity at experiencing such a dramatic and catastrophic loss. He is ashamed of his stupidity; he feels isolated and has no way to go back home.

He also feels betrayed and begins to harbor resentment toward everyone who has actually succeeded in finding their treasure. He decides that his greatest mistake was to believe he could find his treasure in the first place and comes to the conclusion that it is folly to think he could ever change his life or the world. All is vanity, he thinks; nothing can be changed. Santiago is deep into the dark night of his soul.

We should note that an entire third of the story of *The Alchemist* is dedicated to the first stage of Santiago's transformation experience, but in the larger scheme of his lifetime it covers a fairly brief period. The process began with his decision to face his fear of leaving the familiar. His life as a shepherd, and even the flock's dependency on him to meet their basic needs, symbolizes how human nature, left unchallenged, will find the easiest and safest existence. That way, we feel comfortable because we can control, manipulate and work it to our advantage. We think this is a form of power but we will see how it is the antithesis of true empowerment. In addition, we will see, when Santiago made the choice for change, that he was continuously rewarded with a sense of greater empowerment.

Santiago begins with making the choice to pursue inner transformation to find his treasure, using the process as outlined by the alchemists even though he is unaware of alchemy at this point in the story. Fortunately, despite his fiercely independent spirit, Santiago need not make the journey alone. When he is in the desert, seemingly isolated from all his normal support, he will not be as alone as he feels. All the energy of the prima materia—the force that unites all, the unconditional Love at the heart of everything—is devoted to seeing him through the process.

The initial outcome of the black phase for Santiago is an immediate sense of loss, disillusionment and despair. All of the supports of his former life are gone. He was not prepared for this; Melchizedek had not warned him of the painful process he should expect to take place. The depth of this sense of loss is almost understated in the story, but the impact of his loss extends well beyond the incident with the thief who runs off with his money. He feels totally and involuntarily vulnerable.

This is always the impact of the black phase. Loss, despair, vulnerability and most importantly all our fears are exposed.

Fear, when our personality is broken down into the raw ingredients, is one of the most common constituent parts to be revealed. In some cases it can be described as terror or total dread.

Whatever name we give it, entering the black phase will expose the iron grip it has over most aspects of our lives. There is rational fear built into all human nature, which should really be described as caution, and is there for our protection—for example, not putting your hand into fire or keeping your head under water for too long. Then there is irrational fear that lives in the realm of our emotions and triggers certain uncontrollable responses to a variety of life's circumstances and in particular our relationships. This fear can be crippling and at times totally disabling.

The work of the black phase is to expose those fears for what they are, to reveal the power they hold over us and to offer us the opportunity to heal them or, in alchemical terminology, to have them purified. The purification will come in the white phase; the black phase is simply concerned with exposing them.

Getting to the root of our fears is the unavoidable first step of the process of transformation. Unless we can identify the roots of our fears, we will never have them healed and, most importantly, never be able to see them turned into our greatest assets. I say healed because behind every fear is an open wound.

The breakdown of Santiago's normal life support is unavoidable given the choice he has made to find his treasure, and he begins the battle with his decision to stay on the journey. He immediately formulates an alternate plan. He decides there is little point in continuing, because it simply results in repeated loss. He believes his only hope of survival is somehow finding how to recover his former state. Bereft of every significant part of his previous identity, he takes stock of what can get him back to where he came from.

Santiago discovers the stones Melchizedek had given him and considers they had cost him very little. Six sheep in exchange for two stones taken from a breastplate of precious jewels was a good deal. Yet as he continues to ponder on the stones, he decides their value to him is more symbolic than any money he could make by selling them to buy his passage home. They in fact remind him that he had been told to follow the omens when he needed to know the direction to follow to find his treasure.

As his faith in Melchizedek's words returns, he formulates a new attitude. This place of loneliness and despair is not simply a strange place, it is, rather, a new place. Besides, despite the pain that being in this place has already caused him, it's a good place, not a bad place. He accepts that even if he never reaches his final treasure, he has already benefited from the experience.

In his mind he understands that he can choose to wallow in self-pity or accept the challenge of the choices he has made. He decides he is an adventurer, not a victim of his circumstances. He is in control of his destiny. While this may cost him in many ways and he feels as though he has lost his way, he decides to keep going, even if in the end he will be returning to his former situation.

What is fascinating at this point is, Santiago, for the first time, begins to understand the people he has encountered in this new world. They have not changed, but his perception of them has. Most critically, he can more clearly sense people's intentions. His perception of their relationship to the world is heightened. Effortlessly and intuitively, he knows whether they, too, are following their dream. He has discovered an unspoken language between everything in the world—a sixth sense that he has chosen to listen to for the first time. This language will help him to be aware of the omens that Melchizedek described would guide him along his new adventure. His hope is that the omens will lead him back home.

In my experience, the black phase means allowing my consciousness to feel the pain in my unconscious and identify it as the first step toward being able to control its power over me. Yet this is the last thing my conscious self wants to do. Why would I want to revisit pain? Our human programming is to stop pain and run from the hurt, but the consequence is living in fear of it happening again.

What the ancient alchemists discovered, what Jung wrote about and practiced, and what my experience confirms, is that if we do not identify the pain and name it, accept it and allow Love to heal it, then that pain takes control of our lives and hides behind fear. As I know too well, that fear runs most of our lives; and I desperately want to be free from it.

I speak of the black phase in the present tense because together with the white phase and the red phase, these three phases are not a linear experience in the working out of inner alchemy. They form instead a circular experience and are cyclical in their manifestation.

Since I started my personal great work, I have been in each of these phases at different times in the last forty-eight years. The process is continuous until we reach the center, which is the Philosopher's Stone.

I sometimes think of this as the journey of the conscious into the unconscious by way of a series of unlimited, clockwise, spiraling arrows running from the apex of the circumference down to the Philosopher's Stone. Along the way I pass through each of the phases in order of black, white and red. The time I spend in each is determined by a number of factors, as I will discuss here, but it is safe to say, in my experience, it is impossible to move to the next phase before completing them in order.

Following the alchemical process, as I have outlined so far, has enabled me to discover the transformation I longed for. To help explain, I will outline both the inner and practical details. But remember, in alchemy there is no separation between the two. In fact, in my experience, they are one and the same and work in tandem just as they did for the ancient alchemists in their laboratories.

My laboratory is the daily events of my life as I try to transform the base and despised elements of my personality into the most valuable assets I possess, with the aid of Love.

In the following example, I will describe one of the earliest and most important transformation experiments that I conducted. I deliberately started with the black phase, although I did not call it that at the time.

* * *

The root motivation for my decision to engage in this process of transformation was my constant looking for acceptance from others. No matter how hard I tried, I always seemed to be doomed to a lack of self-esteem. Logically, I knew this stemmed from a lack of positive self-love, but that knowledge did not make my overwhelming feeling go away. Most importantly, I also knew the projection onto others of my own buried negativity could destroy any chance I may have for a life of positive, loving relationships.

My greatest discovery, resulting from my choice to enter the black phase and then the white phase, was the child within me. Sadly, I found an inner child who felt deeply unloved, and this was the power he held over the adult me.

The encouraging news is that as a result of the great work I committed to completing, I was able over time to prevent him from dictating my behavior. I want to briefly share how I managed that.

At the time of my commitment, my belief that Love was now

directing my life and would give me the omens to follow my true destiny led me to an amazing community—a family, really—in the south of England. This group believed that if people could experience a caring environment where unconditional love and acceptance was the guiding rule, then Love would bring healing and wholeness into troubled lives. They thought of it as a city of refuge, and I am pleased to say that was my experience.

This was a simple and possibly idealistic concept, but it had a contagious effect on anyone who discovered and shared this aim. Before too long, they attracted other visionaries who came to join them and over a hundred people left their homes around the world and moved into houses in the surrounding area. They were not a new religion or cult, just a community of people who believed in the healing power of Love.

Initially, I joined the group with my young family to support the vision and I was a full-time teacher in a local high school. Over the years we saw miraculous changes happen in wounded people's lives and how the manifestation of Love through human beings brought about that positive change. People who had struggled to get through their daily lives because of emotional obstacles found freedom and the maturity to go on and live productive lives in society. This was powerful stuff!

While I was a member of that community, I made the decision to look again at my inner suffering that still would not go away. Ironically, the more I attempted to live a life of Love toward others, the more I projected my lack of self-love onto them. It was time to see if I could bring some resolve and comfort to my wounded self, and save my relationships.

From within this community I sought out a few people whose wisdom I respected and trusted. I asked if they would be my guides as I embarked on this process. They supported my decision to identify the exact feelings I needed to work with in the healing process. One of them recommended I read the poem "The Dark Night of the Soul" by St. John of the Cross. The original meaning of this "Dark Night" has been reinterpreted by many writers, but the real essence of the saint's poem was accurately captured by Thomas Merton in his book, *Contemplative Prayer*.

Merton, a Trappist monk, who became a lifelong friend of the Dalai Lama, wrote extensively about his personal struggle with faith and his own humanity. He dedicated his life to seeking unity with Love through intense prayer and contemplation. Merton restated the original transformation purpose of St. John of the Cross' poem, which is the deliberate choice to engage in spiritual descent into the dark places of the unconscious and to strip away all self-illusion in relation to faith and the meaning of life.

I read the two books in tandem and made the decision to embark on my own Dark Night of the Soul journey. Merton interpreted the poem in a way I could grasp and helped me to see its beneficial impact as a spiritual exercise. He described the process as a darkening of the feelings and senses resulting in a deep anxiety experienced during contemplative prayer or meditation. He believed this was necessary for anyone wanting to pass the control of our unconscious into the hands of Love and ultimately our conscious self. It marks the lowering of our habitual and conscious defenses because the defenses are limitations. Growth, he explained, will only come from abandoning them. Our conscious defenses are also a protection for our consciousness from the inner dragons of fear that seem too great to face without protection.

Merton went on to say that when we deliberately face and embrace these unconscious forces, our whole belief structure will collapse. He agreed with Jung, who also understood the importance of the black phase, that in the process all of our motives for existence and loving will be smashed to pieces. All of the lights of our life will be extinguished. All of the support values will lose their shape, and we will be plunged into complete darkness—"suspended in the void," as Merton described it.

Even our faith in the reality of Love will be challenged. We are entering into a night in which Love lives without any image: invisible and beyond any mental representation. Our consciousness, he notes, will struggle to hold onto familiar images and concepts of our faith as we descend into the abyss of unknowing towards a new light of deeper reality and truth.

In the terms of the ancient alchemists, the light that St. John, Jung and Merton describe is the Philosopher's Stone and is buried within the center of our being. It is the pearl of great price that Jesus of Nazareth talks about in his parable. The treasure is buried in a field and we have to sell all we possess to buy it. We have to lose everything we think of as valuable to gain the thing of greatest value.

Others advised me in advance that it might be a good idea to take a year off from my demanding teaching job and do something more manual, in case the impact of my inner work meant I might not be able to carry out my classroom responsibilities. This was good advice, and I learned to operate the simple printing press used to publish the community's monthly magazine.

I was expecting I would need more emotional space in my life and yet I was not prepared for what happened. The dark night of my soul was about as black as can be imagined.

Those I trusted to catch me when I fell were right on every count about the depth of the fall I should expect, and I fell a long way down. My shock at entering the unconscious was a totally debilitating experience.

To be clear, this was not a bout of depression; I am fortunate to have never been a depressed person. Nor was it the result of a life changing trauma resulting in loss or grief. As strange as it may seem, I deliberately chose to pass through this process with the conviction that I had enough faith in transformation and the power of Love to reach the treasure I sought: the freedom to Love myself and others unconditionally.

The daily form of my transforming process took on a simple

routine. I would wake early and then, instead of spending my waking moments daydreaming or letting my mind wander toward all the plans of the day, I would recite a short formulaic prayer commonly used by the Eastern Churches. For me, the purpose of the prayer was to prevent the clutter of my conscious thoughts dominating my mind; that way, when I later spent time in silent contemplation, I was more easily able to work with the feelings that arose.

What I would recite over and over was my version of the *Jesus Prayer:*

"Lord have mercy on me. Christ have mercy on me. Lord Jesus Christ, have mercy on me."

That was my mantra for a whole twelve months of my life. Whenever I was tempted to fall into my usual thought patterns, I would discipline my mind to return to the *Jesus Prayer.*

For the rest of the morning, I would focus on the tasks of everyday family life as well as running the simple printing press. It was a repetitive job and saved the community money by not having to pay professional printers to produce a monthly magazine. For me, it was a simpler life than having to teach demanding teenagers in a busy high school.

At lunchtime I would take a basic meal and sit alone inside the local village parish church when it was cold or on the grounds of the church in summer. It was during these times, when I was away from everyone else, that I would enter my unconscious in the spirit of contemplative prayer and allow all the despised fears and feelings buried within the darkness of my soul to have a voice.

It was a dark and traumatic time! Just as Merton had predicted, I faced losing all of the conscious supports of faith and doctrine that had held me up in the past few years. With the passage of each day, week and month, my soul was being stripped bare of all sense of who I was, the good and the bad; in its place was a deep feeling of total emptiness.

If my goal was to descend into the pit of hopelessness, then this was certainly working. As each day passed, I allowed myself to feel the inner pain of loneliness, despair and abandonment. These were the core feelings of my unconscious, and I knew I would never be truly free to seize all that life had to offer me — and enter into my true destiny — unless I owned the components of my inner darkness. I was highly motivated at the start, but as time passed even that motivation came into question. "What," asked my conscious mind, "is the point of it all?"

The slate upon which all my goals and dreams were written was being wiped clean, and at the time nothing was being written in their place.

The cultural and conditional premises that gave my life meaning, such as the desire to help and improve the lives of others, disintegrated. I discovered my self-esteem was built on how helpful I was to those around me, and that desire soon vanished too. I saw that my illusionary self-image desperately needed to die a slow and painful death, and that beneath that was the void I previously had tried to avoid. Now I stared down into it and asked, "Who am I really?"

Eventually, after several months, the profound answer came back loud and clear: "You are the abandoned and wounded child who needs a voice to become whole."

I met with my two life support mentors weekly to monitor my progress and share my reports. They were experienced enough to understand what I was encountering and encouraged me to continue as long as I felt strong enough. Only one of them had also tried to do what I was doing, with mixed results. He had managed to reach into the depths of his unconscious using this Dark Night of the Soul technique but was still struggling to heal the wounds he had uncovered. I remember thinking — true to my nature — that if I stuck with my own process, maybe one of my outcomes could be my offering to help him.

There were times, however, when my life felt completely devoid of any encouraging signs to keep going. Even carrying the feelings of emptiness day to day was almost too great a burden to bear.

Despite all this, somehow I found the strength to stick with it. After about six months, I recall a glimmer of light beginning to appear in my consciousness. A small miracle was taking place in my daily life as I plunged into my inner depths. Slowly and without my being immediately conscious of it, I found I was beginning to believe I was loved for who I was by those closest to me.

The weak and wounded child within, whom I had now exposed to my conscious self, was feeling loved and accepted unconditionally by others, even if I had not reached that point of self-love just yet. This encouraged me enough to keep going, as hard as it was.

But this was where I reached the lowest point of the black phase, as I now call it. The real and controlling feelings of my unconscious were identified and exposed and now needed purification and cleansing. It was time for the white phase.

For Your Consideration

The choice to deliberately face your dragons is potentially one of the most painful experiences you will ever know; but if you do not do this, life will often force you into the experience as an unwilling participant. Grief is a primary example of a forced event that will easily unlock the unconscious. We will all experience loss at some point in our lives; it is built into the fabric of human existence and cannot be avoided. The death of loved ones, a traumatic event or accident, rejection, disease or a debilitating physical illness, war and severe poverty—all these major life events trigger grief. The loss of what we once had can be life changing, and many people never recover and regain a positive momentum in their emotional lives. The fact that many do is the miracle of the resilient power within the human spirit, but it is also a sad truth that many do not.

The alchemists knew this and believed that the miracle of transformation, from the darkness of despair to the light of new hope, could be an active process which we choose to embrace. They also believed transformation was not possible without the involvement of Love, because in the darkness of despair the only hope we have is that Love is there with us, invisible and yet present.

In the famous words of St. Paul the Apostle:

"For now we see through a glass, darkly; but then face to face: now I know in part; but then shall I know even as also I am known. And now abideth faith, hope, charity, these three; but the greatest of these is charity."
(1 Cor.12-13).

This *King James Version* translates the Greek word *agape* as "charity", as distinct from the generic English word for love. If we correctly define charity as the unconditional giving of help to someone in need, then this is exactly what we will need in the black phase. In fact, we will need all the help from Love we can get, and by any means possible.

The path of facing the reality of truth about ourselves and discovering integrity is too hard for many to walk. Most of us build lives avoiding or ignoring such deep inner pain. However, if we attempt to stay within the comfortable and the convenient and do not go into the shadow, the shadow will always come into our consciousness when it is not convenient—and make us, very, very uncomfortable.

In other words, if you do not go into the shadow and face the dragons, you will end up there anyway through the normal course of your life; and this time the dragons will be in control.

Facing the dragons in the darkness of your unconscious is, in my experience, the only option if you are seeking a life of purpose, wholeness and true empowerment.

Facing the dragons puts you in control of your destiny.

If you trust Love sufficiently to make that inner alchemical journey, then the reward of true empowerment awaits and instantly kicks into action. Love is literally waiting for us just to say, "Yes!" Once you do so, you will discover a supernatural courage to identify and embrace those parts of yourself you have spent your life rejecting.

No two journeys will be same. You live a unique life and have your own dragons to face. But the universal truth is that the transformation of your despised self into your greatest treasure is eternal.

Love, if you have the eyes to see it, has gone before to pave the way.

Omens are all around to encourage you through the process. You do not need to face the dragons in the darkness alone, because in that place you will discover that Love has already accepted everything about you, and wants you to transform in every aspect of your life. Love wants to enfold you.

I make my promise again: I have asked Love to give you everything you need to be the alchemist in your world as you pass through the black phase of your journey.

Chapter 7

Working in the Crystal Shop

In the preceding chapter I discussed not only the need for the painful black phase but also the importance of the breaking down of our inner self into its constituent parts before we can progress with transformation towards true empowerment. Once that process is achieved, we are ready to enter the white phase, where we take those ingredient parts of ourselves and refine them. After the night of darkness, we will slowly move to the light of a new dawn. We will have seen the gradual death of the power of those needs that controlled our lives. Old dependencies, beliefs and habits will lose their grip and a new transformed person will emerge. To follow the way of the ancient alchemists and for transformation to continue, we will need to work with the remnants from the black phase.

In their laboratories, what the alchemists did next with the matter that survived was critical for the alchemical process to continue toward the manifestation of gold. This included a cleansing or washing of the elements and reforming them into new, purer matter. If they did not fulfill this part of the process, then their ability to produce gold would be contaminated.

Moreover, in our inner transformation process we will potentially get stuck in the black phase and spend the rest of our lives buried under the pieces of our inner self.

"He or she is a shell of their former self," is a common description of someone who has experienced a major trauma. This is not a place where we are meant to stay. If we do, then true empowerment will remain beyond our reach or at best be severely limited.

The good news is the white phase is not full of the pain and seeming death or fear of the black phase. There is light at the end of this tunnel, and a growing sense of rebirth and new life will emerge. This phase will include a commitment to some hard work, but the rewards come thick and fast to encourage us to press on toward the treasure.

The ancient alchemists discovered another interesting phenomenon in the white phase: a fundamental duality in the very nature of matter. The remaining elements to be purified contained seemingly opposing qualities. They found positive and negative characteristics, which they identified as male and female: the king and queen or sun and moon. The significance of this discovery is crucially important to the successful completion of the white phase.

The white phase is not only about purification but also unification. Together with their work in the laboratory, the ancient alchemist had to merge the inner opposing powers, the male and female. It was in that unity, that inseparable joining together, that producing gold was achieved; and with it came a new level of integrity and strength. This is another property of the Philosopher's Stone.

To make practical sense of this, the alchemists divided the purification process into two parts: separation and conjunction. Separation enabled the alchemist to finally isolate the nature of the real inner person they had freed from the control of the needs of the unconscious self and the pretense of the conscious self.

In other words, healing and wholeness can take the place of a divided self.

In graphic form the ancient alchemists often represented this as a sword ready to cut open that which was concealed, and so expose it to light and air. Having identified the parts of potential value, they could raise them to a higher plane of enlightenment. In the white phase, that which we despised and rejected as having no value is allowed to grow towards the light of Love.

Conjunction now follows separation, with those revalued parts recombined to form new matter. In alchemical symbolism, this is also the union of the four elements of Fire, Air and Water to produce a new Earth. The new earth element is the child of the conjunction, a conception of new life through the love between the male and female of the inner self. The alchemists called this the "sacred marriage". No longer opposing each other, the king and queen, sun and moon, unite to create the fetus, or the "lesser stone". Jung's view was that at this stage, the ancient alchemist should or would nurture this new child into becoming the mature adult or, using Jung's term, the "self". This is the "greater stone", the Philosopher's Stone.

Sometimes the laboratory process of "separation" and "conjunction" is shown in alchemical drawings as two birds initially facing opposite directions, representing the disconnection of the spirit and the soul. However, when the true elements of the self did combine, no one, not even the ancient alchemist, knew what new person would emerge. What they did know, however, was that the combination of the male and female would produce a child with a new consciousness, dominated by neither the patriarchal nor the matriarchal elements.

This philosopher's child is in essence a higher intuitive being. She or he combines the thirst for action of the male with the heartfelt passion of the female; this union of thought and feeling lives in a state of reality and integrity.

Remember that the goal is refinement of the incorruptible Philosopher's Stone. In Jungian terms, as we have seen, the process of individuation produces a new self, Jung's name for the philosopher's child that can manage whatever realities life and nature throw at it and still survive untainted. No manner of confused thoughts, overwhelming emotions and the negative behavior of others will destroy the solid refuge that is our personal stone. This is the inner home of confidence and integrity that Jung believed was the birthright of everyone. This is the birthplace and home of true empowerment.

* * *

During Santiago's experience of being robbed in the marketplace, he was distracted by the most beautiful sword he had ever seen. It had a silver embossed scabbard with precious gems embedded into the handle. This occurs just before he enters the black phase of total loss and is an omen he finds attractive but does not yet recognize.

The sword represents the white phase he is about to enter. He wants the sword badly enough to promise that one day he will buy it, and yet it is never mentioned again in the story. The sword is a metaphorical symbol of the white phase, in which the concealed fears of his unconscious will be cut open and exposed to the desert sun, thus leading the way to the unified self.

Santiago makes his way up a hill in the town where he passes a store selling glass crystal. He is penniless and hungry. He notices the window display is dirty and offers to clean it for the merchant in exchange for some food. The merchant says nothing, so Santiago quickly starts cleaning the glassware anyway. As he does, two customers enter to make a purchase: the only sale of the morning.

Santiago seizes on the opportunity to replace the money he has lost by offering to work all day and night cleaning the rest of the stock in the shop to earn the means to continue toward the pyramids. To Santiago's surprise, however, the merchant says that even if he cleans the glass for a year and earns commission on every sale, he will not make enough to take him to Egypt. The pyramids were a long way across the desert, and hoping to make enough money to get there was completely unrealistic.

Santiago is thrown into a deep state of total disappointment at this news. His last vestige of hope, which would have kept him moving toward finding his treasure, is extinguished; his soul is silent. The hopelessness of his situation brings him to the point of contemplating that death itself might be easier than the despair he feels in that moment.

The merchant watches Santiago's reaction and kindly offers the money for his passage back to Andalusia. But after a few moments, with all hope of finding his treasure gone, Santiago tells the merchant he will work for him so he can buy more sheep when he gets back home. He will go home to be a shepherd again.

For a whole year Santiago, driven by his decision to head back to where he once belonged, works enthusiastically in the shop selling the glass crystal. He pours all his energy into helping the merchant make his business a success, and the results are rewarding for both Santiago and the merchant. The business has been transformed by selling tea in the crystal. The customers are drawn to the shop by the beauty of the glassware and the magical way it lifts their spirits.

In addition to making plenty of money to fulfill his new plan to buy his passage home and buy more sheep than he had ever owned, Santiago discovers an important lesson from the merchant: most people choose not to pursue their dreams.

Just so, the merchant's fear of failure had been greater than his desire to follow his dream. To avoid the disappointment of not being successful, the merchant had chosen not to try to be successful. He preferred to dream of going to Mecca, an obligation of his religion, rather than actually trying to make that journey.

His excuse to himself was that no one could look after his business while he was away, so there was a danger that he would lose everything when making the trip. For the merchant the dream of going to Mecca had replaced the effort he needed to make the money to actually make the pilgrimage. For that reason, the merchant had failed to make the needed changes in the shop which would have made it profitable. And yet, now here was Santiago, pointing out the potential of the business.

The merchant understood that if he allowed Santiago to make the business a financial success the one excuse he had for not following his dream would be removed. Despite his deep-seated fear of not achieving success, he allowed Santiago to make the changes.

With Santiago's entrepreneurial efforts, the crystal shop becomes a financial success beyond either of their expectations. As a result, within a year Santiago had sufficient money not only to afford his passage home but also to reconsider setting out after all on his journey to find his treasure.

The merchant knew that he would probably never make his pilgrimage but that Santiago would continue his journey because now he was ready; and it was his destiny. *"Maktub,"* he tells Santiago, "It is written."

Santiago's time in the crystal shop is a clear metaphor for his entering the alchemical white phase of cleansing and purification. The shop is his unconscious, and the merchant is the voice within it.

When we understand that *The Alchemist* is a handbook on alchemy, this particular episode in the story takes on a whole new significance. In this instance the story's brilliance is in taking the extremely difficult topic of listening and identifying the voice in the unconscious by portraying it cleverly within the metaphor of the glass crystal.

The glass is dirty and unattractive, and no one wants to buy it. Santiago commits to cleaning and has instantly edifying results; and the more he cleans, the more people are attracted to it. He reaches the point where people even want to drink from these clean crystal glasses and will pay for the privilege. It becomes the most successful shop of its kind in the town.

If the crystal shop represents Santiago's unconscious, the glass is a symbol for those parts of his personality remaining after the black phase. This is the raw matter of his very being that now needs to be purified. Each piece of crystal needs careful handling when being cleaned so it does not break. Then it is put on display to reveal its worth to others. If you own an expensive piece of cut crystal glass, you will know that to show it off to its best advantage it needs to be placed in sunlight or under a spotlight. When spotless and in the light, the true magic of the crystal cutter's work is revealed.

The glass crystal represents the need to take the delicate and seemingly unattractive parts of our unconscious and expose them to the light of Love. The light will only work its magic if we are prepared to do the work of exposing those parts, treating them with respect and then displaying the results.

What is easy to miss in the crystal metaphor is that the glass is made with lead oxide. Lead crystal is known for its clarity and is the popular choice for beautiful chandeliers, sparking dress jewelry and fine wine glasses. The higher the lead content in crystal, the greater the clarity.

When Santiago is cleaning the crystal in the shop, he is symbolically taking the base parts of his inner self, represented by the lead in the glass, and refining them so they become objects of great beauty and worth. This corresponds to the ancient alchemists' work in the white phase; to succeed, it required the utmost dedication and focus. This was the critical stage in the great work of the alchemist, and the white phase continues until all the base parts have been cherished and can lovingly reveal their priceless and unique characteristics.

Also, in this metaphor the merchant's voice is that of Santiago's unconscious. As Santiago performs the cleansing and purification process, the voice first expresses regret and then fear of change. Santiago's unconscious has relinquished the ability to hope and dream of a better future. It has decided its fears cannot be overcome and has resigned itself to the way things are. The wounds and pain of failure are too great to bear. For this reason, Santiago's unconscious does not want to change its old ways and habits.

However, Santiago's cleansing work is forcing his unconscious voice to dare to be positive, to hope and to face the amazing possibilities that he could achieve if only he could overcome his fears.

Santiago hears this voice and chooses to continue with the work of cleansing until he has enough of value to continue his life. Eventually the voice moves from its initial position of resignation to being willing to take the risk of failure. The purification has worked!

Interestingly, Santiago's work in the crystal shop lasts eleven months and nine days. In traditional numerology the number eleven represents awakening, illumination and enlightenment. The number nine has long been associated with endings that are set to bring about new and spiritually transformed beginnings. It also represents leadership, service to humanity and the spiritual laws that govern the universe. It is not surprising that the story refers to these numbers to heighten the significance of the end of the white phase for Santiago: he is empowered to move on to complete his destiny.

At the end of his time in the crystal shop, Santiago emerges wearing expensive white linen Arabian clothing: new clothes for a new man. In his hand is more money than he has ever owned. The main work of cleansing and purifying the base elements of his unconscious is complete, and he is ready to move on and be successful at whatever he finally chooses—to be a shepherd again or to go forward and continue to the next phase of the alchemical process. Either way, his life is no longer ruled by fear. His mind is now open to new possibilities.

* * *

For me, the challenge that came at the end of the black phase meant I had to work on how to heal the wounded child within. But at least I now knew the child existed, and that awareness immediately diffused much of the destructive power the child had over me. If the process of transformation were to be successful, and the wounded child healed and matured to help me reach my treasure, then something radical needed to happen.

At this point I decided to let the wounded child within me plead directly with Love for help. My adult self was so stripped of any hope of finding an answer that during my contemplative sessions I stepped out of the way and let the child himself reach out. I let him use his voice. Fortunately, considering the volume and intensity of that voice of his, I was usually alone and out of hearing distance during these lunchtime sessions.

If the child needed to scream, I let him scream. If he needed to sob, I let him sob. If he wanted an angry rant, I let him rant. These were private affairs between my wounded child and Love, and I had no idea how that relationship was going to turn out. I just knew it needed to happen, and my mentors seemed to agree it was a good idea.

This exercise was based in part on Gestalt therapy, developed mostly in the United States by Fritz and Laura Perls along with Paul Goodman in the 1940s and 1950s. Their therapeutic method focused on giving voice to real feelings in a controlled environment with a therapist, rather than venting them in real situations day to day where they may cause harm. (See Talia Levine Bar-Yoseph's fascinating work on the subject in *Gestalt Therapy: Advances in Theory and Practice*.)

The core Gestalt philosophy lies in accepting feelings for what they are, giving them a voice and then seeking to address them, rather than leaving them pent up. In practice, it involves facing an empty chair and imagining the angry child who needs to give vent to what he or she feels sitting there. Ideally then, the adult self can enable the child to feel heard, and a resulting conversation can be had to help resolve whatever was not resolved in childhood. In my case, I had very little to offer my "child in the chair", so I let Love have the conversation; and Love said it was fine for the child to be angry because the anger was the result of a deep wound.

Love not only heard my wounded child but sent practical help which significantly advanced my journey in the person of Dr. Frank Lake, a respected British psychiatrist who later wrote masterfully on this subject in *Clinical Theology: A Theological and Psychiatric Basis to Clinical Pastoral Care.*

Lake was invited to speak at one of the mini-conferences held by the community to which I belonged. He believed he had discovered the means to heal deep wounds inflicted during early childhood or even before birth. I was all ears!

During his professional studies, Lake had adopted the psychodynamic theory which advocates that most psychic problems have their origin in traumatic experiences inflicted in earliest infancy. From 1954 onwards, in India, where he had been commissioned as a psychiatric missionary, Lake began treating patients by using hyperventilation or deep breathing to induce memories of early childhood traumas. By opening the gate to the unconscious, he recorded patients reliving emotional childhood traumas. His results generally confirmed the theories of Jung's psychoanalysis. However, the therapeutic work of Lake and other renowned psychiatrists surpassed Jung's psychoanalysis in speed and results.

When Lake returned to England and continued his work, he discovered something even more incredible: patients were going back in time to earlier experiences than childhood and birth, even being in the womb. He now termed his technique *Primal Integration,* within his theory of *Clinical Theology.* His hypothesis, born out in some amazingly successful case studies with patients, postulated that various kinds of common emotional problems—anxiety experienced in close human relations, as well as feelings of abandonment, dependency, phobias and fears of death, including even falling and being crushed—may have their origin in the birth and womb experience. But it was possible, Lake discovered, to integrate and release this buried pain by simulating the birth and womb experience in a controlled therapy session.

I recall Lake saying in his presentation that an intelligent recreation of the conditions of birth and a reliving of the ordeal by simulation were desperately needed if any integration of trauma was to be achieved. I heard my inner child shout: "Amen to that!" Immediately I signed up for my first primal integration session with Lake, which was scheduled the following weekend at my community.

Lake had developed practical methods to integrate not only the trauma of birth but also earlier negative fetal experiences. He began the therapeutic session with a verbal induction in the form of a Fantasy Journey, a mild form of self-hypnosis that enabled me to quickly recall my earliest experiences. Using this method gave the control to me as the patient, and I was able to regulate the depth of my experience. Using the deep, intensive breathing of hyperventilation, I was able to dive back into my experience of birth and pre-birth fetal memories.

In my session I recall Lake explaining that the fetus possibly receives the worst traumas during the first trimester of the gestation period, typically around the experience of conception, the fallopian tube journey, implantation, and then later as an embryo, birthing and bonding. Not everyone in that session found these recalled experiences traumatic; in fact, one friend of mine found the whole reliving of his pre-birth and birth experience a wonderful joyride of great happiness. Unfortunately, that was not true in my case.

Without disclosing all the details of my experience, it is safe to say I went through the full gamut of emotions: sadness, exhaustion, anger, fear and anxiety. Over two or three sessions I felt gloomy desolation and burst into tears on a regular basis. I also expressed furious rage by pounding a pillow with my fists. Lake had insisted that I must have two facilitators sitting with me in my session. These helpers were people I deeply trusted; they helped me maintain contact with my adult ego state and advised me to release all surfacing emotions and give them free expression.

In addition to these emotions, I experienced a deep physical coldness and numbness all along the left side of my body. My facilitators encouraged me to let this intensify—to open myself up to this sensation and dive into it. When I deliberately focused on my pain, I immediately began to feel nauseous and started to vomit. Clearly, to me, my fetal self was trying to reject something unwanted but which seemed to be invading me. Lake then encouraged me to use my imagination and willpower to drive this sensation of being invaded down my left side towards the navel and out of my body via the imaginary fallopian tube. In my mind I was ejecting a black fluid, almost akin to poison.

Once I completed this final primal integration session, I felt completely weak and exhausted. Lake and my facilitators gathered round me to ask Love to replace the painful sensation with eternal Love and compassion. I recall apologizing at great length for them having to witness my mess and them saying how they were thrilled I was able to get in touch with those feelings!

After that session, what I experienced was that, for the second time in my life, my whole being was infused with Love, but this time in a significantly different way. This was not a flush of enlightenment as it had felt at the time of my encounter with Love; this time it was an abiding, deep sense of wellbeing, a solid knowledge in my very core that Love was in control.

The following days and weeks led into the constructive white phase. I was now able to work with the wounded child who had finally stopped his raging and demands. He had found his voice and had my cooperation and understanding. Most importantly, he had my compassion. Together we could now face life and work out what he else he needed to assist me in the quest for my treasure.

Not long after my final primal integration session, I decided I would have to visit my mother to find answers for some unanswered questions that had emerged from my sessions. Was what I had experienced based on real events? I was very eager to find out.

I took care to choose the right moment to visit her and decided not to scare her with the details of my therapeutic session. My wife had meanwhile filled in some gaps in my knowledge based on comments my mother had shared with her.

I casually asked my mother about her time being pregnant with me.

Based on what my mother said, we were able to conclude that I was an only child because she had experienced two ectopic pregnancies after I was born. That had caused her doctors to conclude it was a miracle I had made it to full term. Further, they had told her that for her own safety's sake, she should not attempt any further pregnancies. It seems that during her second trimester carrying me, she had suffered blood poisoning, or septicemia, from an unknown cause. Apparently both my mother and I almost died from this; we survived thanks to penicillin. This news possibly explained the sensation I experienced in my primal integration session: the blood poisoning could have been the fetal invasion I had sensed.

Fortunately, my birth was uncomplicated. But all my mother's attempts to breastfeed me failed, and apparently both of us became very anxious until I was fed on replacement milk.

Then, within a few months of birth, I contracted whooping cough and came close to death once again, when I would have periods of not breathing at all. My parents and grandparents took turns nursing me round the clock for two weeks to make sure I kept breathing.

Sadly, my mother suffered her own side effects from my birth, which were to have repercussions on my early life. To the surprise of everyone (including me), when I was two years old she started to have epileptic fits. I have one vague but truly traumatic memory of an incident when I was a toddler in our small first home. I recall her rolling on the floor with blood on her face, a neighbor running in and paramedics arriving to take her to hospital—just as my father arrived home from work to take care of me.

My mother was given medication and electric shock treatments to control the severe fits, but none of that stopped her occasional smaller seizures (known medically as absence seizures) and bouts of unpredictable behavior. When still only a toddler, she would be speaking to me in a loving way, and then, for no reason, verbally abuse me and lock me in a dark cupboard under the stairs. A couple of hours later, or so it seemed to me, she would open the cupboard and chastise me for hiding in there, apparently completely unaware of what had just happened.

At other times, during one of her uncontrolled outbursts, she would blame me for her being the way she was. When this behavior was eventually discovered by my father, she was thankfully given drugs to control it by her doctor. Life slowly improved for us all.

I had spent a lifetime not knowing these details. What uncovering all this did for me was that finally I was able to piece together the story of my earliest beginnings. This gave me the ability to embrace my confused and demanding child. I was now able to stand back and understand why that child felt attacked and abused by the one person who should have provided love and protection.

I was equally able to help that child see that none of this was his or his mother's fault. The child and my adult self were able to look at my mother with new eyes of compassion instead of fear, anger, disappointment and resentment. My adult relationship with my mother changed for the better—beyond recognition, in fact.

Later in life I was able to help nurse her back from a major brain operation, when she finally understood the cause of her epilepsy. An arteriovenous malformation burst within her brain was removed by an expert surgeon. She spent the last twenty-five years of her life finally free from medication and the fear of fits.

This primal integration had set me free to start a process in which I was able to forgive her and give comfort to the child she so desperately wanted to nurture. I was now in the white phase, and all the hard work I had put into the black phase was finally paying off.

When I later told Dr. Frank Lake about the septicemia in my fetal stage, he was thrilled about the positive connection as a result of our session. He told me he believed I had vomited out the memory of the poison and asked if he could include it in his case studies.

The key progress for the adult me was the ability to move forward and reorient my life within a new positive reality. Instead of rejecting the wounded child within, I embraced his incredible strength to survive. He had a courage and determination I could draw on. He had miraculously survived life-threatening dangers and unexplained rejection through most of his early life.

Of all the outcomes that primal integration delivered, the most startling discovery I made was something I absolutely never expected: my wounded child's strength came from an existing relationship with Love that was unique, intimate and fully integrated into who he was. My wounded child was not separated from Love; he was enfolded in Love. This was an overwhelming truth that not even the exponents of the dark night of the soul had intimated would be my experience.

I had assumed that there was only pain, suffering, ugliness, fear and devastation in the darkest place of my soul, and I had expected it would be my adult self's job to make good and repair the damage. On the contrary, however, when I discovered the truth of who I really was, I discovered a victor, not a victim: a king, not a pauper—a fully integrated soul full of the light of Love. I was all these things not because my beginnings were perfect, but because they were imperfect. My strength came from being one with all things: bedded in truth, not fantasy and dependent on Love, not circumstance. I had truly found what the ancient alchemists called the philosopher's child.

This was the end of my white phase, and the way forward meant I no longer needed others to prove to me that I was worthy of Love. I did not need their affirmation, and my need for it no longer colored my relationships. I was free to love myself and to love others without wanting anything in return. I was on the path to being able to love unconditionally.

I was ready for the red phase of transformation, which would lead toward the manifestation of my newly discovered empowerment.

For Your Consideration

Most people that I have been privileged to help along their paths of transformation have at some point encountered a wounded child within. Not all, but most. If you are one of the fortunate ones for whom early childhood developmental stages have been filled with only positive and life enhancing experiences, then this is an immense gift and reduces the need to face considerable trauma in the black phase.

For most of us, the wounded child is also one of the greatest gifts of our lives because when we make the commitment to meet our child, who is at one with Love, we can be propelled along the way toward our treasure.

The white phase for me was about taking the feelings identified in the black phase and discovering their root cause. Not all modern psychiatrists would advocate this approach in my own interpretation of the alchemical process. In recent decades, most professional counselors and psychiatrists have followed the behavioral or cognitive perspective, so if you, the reader, have been diagnosed with a mental health concern, then seeking out professional help is the first step you should take to finding relief.

The process I am describing in this book is not a substitute for professional consultation; my experience encourages another perspective that can work in tandem with medically accepted approaches to treating mental health problems. Your professional health specialist is best placed to advise you on alternative approaches.

The alchemical process I have used in my life has worked for me because of the spiritual perspective I wanted to bring to finding the solution to what I believed was holding me back from living life to the full. I share it here with you in the hope that it may be of some value.

Specifically, I am not advocating that the only way through the black phase is to follow the dark night of the soul or that the white phase needs to include primal integration. There is no single formula to finding your own treasure and true empowerment. Whichever practical process you choose, it will be part of your true destiny and at a high level will always follow a process of breaking down, followed by purification and then forward empowerment.

Based on the reality of my own journey, I have consciously included Love in this process. If your life perspective includes the goal of achieving true empowerment, then for you the white phase will require a purification of your whole self. This may include approaching the wounded child within, in which case my advice is to seek out a counselor who can specifically assist, at least in an understanding of your possible early childhood experiences of deprivation and abuse.

Most professional counselors are open to discussing this as a means of working with the effect of those episodes on your adult behavior and relationship issues. The white phase is a healing moment, and the most critical part of that is the integration of your adult self with the hidden, denied and despised child in the unconscious.

This is the time when negative and disabling thoughts and attitudes that dominate your adult life can be faced and embraced. There is no other way to be transformed in the renewal of the mind. The goal is to turn "I can't!" into "I can!" and "I don't have a future!" into "The future is mine!"

During this time in the white phase, I offer the guiding thoughts that kept me going through the most difficult of times: there is a light at the end of the tunnel, and Love is there all the time guiding us to the point of our liberation.

I have asked Love to deliver you, the reader, through your white phase to give you the empowerment your heart yearns for.

Chapter 8

There Will be Blood

"When the alchemist sees the perfect whiteness, the philosophers say that one has to destroy his books, because they have become superfluous."
Dom Pernety (1716–1796).

The third part of the traditional alchemical process of transformation is the red phase. The ancient alchemists saw this as the stage where the purified elements created in their laboratory during the white phase could now release powerful energy into this final stage of the physical experiment.

They often chose to represent the transition between the two phases in the form of the White Queen and the Red King, who can be seen in illustrations holding a container together. In the laboratory this unification is achieved through turning up the heat on the experiment. (See R. Swinburne Clymer's *Hermetic Science And Alchemical Process*.)

Jung maintained in *Psychology and Alchemy* that this was a daybreak moment, the quietness and peace of dawn before the full glory of the sunrise. The alchemist, who was also working on inner transformation, at this point would often feel exhausted and depleted because the impure energies of the former self have been removed and it was now time for the new energy to be injected. This new energy comes from the union of the queen and king, and the result will be the birth of the philosopher's child. As we have seen earlier, this child carried a new state of awareness, well beyond a feminine or masculine view of the world.

In alchemy, the queen and king represent the two core spiritual forces at the heart of everything in the cosmos. The feminine and the masculine in all things. The feminine living in the soul and the masculine abiding in the spirit. This is also the marriage of the sun and moon. The red hue of the blood moon, caused by the total eclipse of the sun by the moon, is another alchemical symbol in this phase.

The red phase is also interpreted by Christian alchemists of the past as the process of the resurrection. In their faith understanding, the body of Christ has been crucified, then descended into hell, and is now turned into resurrected immortal oneness with the Father, completed by ascension into heaven. This is the unity of earth and heaven, fire and water: the creation of the new kingdom. As for his part in the transformation, the Christian alchemist, by receiving the Holy Spirit, puts on a new body.

In his laboratory, the ancient alchemist would use intense heat to subject the chemical matter to fermentation, distillation and coagulation. This is comparable to first creating wine and then turning it into spirits. The final product was the channeling of the solidified matter into its final purified form. The chemical coagulation and the spiritual forces, together, create the Philosopher's Stone. This is the ancient alchemist's holy grail of the great work.

At a spiritual level the ancient alchemists attested to a new state of being. They often described this as a completely healed human who had burned away the dross and was free to fly, unencumbered by the mental and cultural constraints of the former self. But they were all aware of one critical part of the process. For the Philosopher's Stone to be produced, their personal transformation needed to occur simultaneously with the success of the red phase of the physical experiment.

It is worth noting here that all the key alchemical processes I have explained so far are summarized on the mystical Emerald Tablet, a mythical emerald crystal gemstone engraved with the inscription below. It was the most revered source document of the ancient alchemists. The origins of the tablet supposedly dated back to the early Egyptian Thoth writings. It will come as no surprise that the actual green crystalline stone has been lost to antiquity, but its mythical inscription has been preserved through the ages by ancient alchemist scholars. Isaac Newton made a translation from these sources, and a copy of it was discovered among his alchemical papers, currently housed in King's College Library in Cambridge, England.

The translation reads:

"Tis true without lying, certain and most true. That which is below is like that which is above and that which is above is like that which is below to do the miracles of one only thing. And as all things have been and arose from one by the mediation of one: so all things have their birth from this one thing by adaptation. The Sun is its father, the moon its mother, the wind hath carried it in its belly, the earth is its nurse. The father of all perfection in the whole world is here. Its force or power is entire if it be converted into earth. Separate thou the earth from the fire, the subtle from the gross sweetly with great industry. It ascends from the earth to the heaven and again it descends to the earth and receives the force of things superior and inferior. By this means you shall have the glory of the whole world & thereby all obscurity shall fly from you. Its force is above all force. For it vanquishes every subtle thing & penetrates every solid thing. So was the world created. From this are & do come admirable adaptations whereof the means (or process) is here in this. Hence I am called Hermes Trismegist, having the three parts of the philosophy of the whole world. That which I have said of the operation of the Sun is accomplished and ended."

(Isaac Newton. "Keynes MS. 28," The Chymistry of Isaac Newton.)

Jung identified the Emerald Tablet with a table made of green stone which he encountered in the first of his dreams and visions beginning at the end of 1912. In the terminology of Jung's *Analytical Psychology*, the red phase encompasses the final stages of the individuation process, where the unconscious and the conscious join and become integrated into a well-functioning whole. It is also what makes each person unique.

When this process is complete, the new self is able to move on to live a productive life to the full extent of its innate and learned talents and skills. The unconscious and the conscious are unified, and the new person can become an active participant in society, enjoying a life of meaningful relationships and experiencing purpose and contentment through passion.

* * *

Not long after leaving the Crystal Shop, Santiago had his first conscious encounter with the world of alchemy by way of the Englishman and his books. Santiago met the Englishman when he decided to join a camel caravan headed for the pyramids. Santiago expected little from the journey across the vast expanse of the desert, except to arrive in Egypt and hopefully to have his treasure revealed. He had never heard of alchemy and was certainly not expecting that the lessons he would learn on the journey would be the way to eventually find his treasure.

We discover the Englishman had for years vainly been seeking to produce the Philosopher's Stone. Despite all his studies and his attempts to gain assistance from people who called themselves alchemists, he consistently had been blocked in his progress. His last remaining hope was to find an Arabian alchemist who was said to live at an oasis along the route to the pyramids. But the Englishman did not expect to become a tutor to Santiago in the ways of alchemy. His attention, however, is drawn from his books when he sees Santiago playing with his Umin and Thummim stones. And so an ongoing conversation begins between the two, in which the Englishman reveals all he knows about the ancient alchemists' craft.

During the early part of their journey together, they discuss the importance of omens, luck and coincidence. The Englishman explains to Santiago the meaning of The Soul of the World, and how we are close to it when we follow our heart's desire. He describes how all things are connected through The Soul of the World; mineral and vegetable and even human thought itself.

He instructs Santiago in the importance of transformation and how everything that exists is continuously in a transformative process. He goes on to introduce Santiago to the ancient alchemists and their theories, including the details of The Emerald Tablet, The Master Work, The Elixir of Life, and finally, the Philosopher's Stone, with its power to turn lead into gold.

In return Santiago describes what he is learning through his conversations with the camel driver about the desert and the caravan's progress through it. He tells the Englishman he can see the soul of the desert and the soul of the caravan speak to each other. He says he now knows that this is The Language of the World. However, neither Santiago nor the Englishman are able to appreciate the value of the other's approach, and they eventually abandon their attempts to learn from each other.

At this point they arrive at the oasis.

The significance of the oasis for the Englishman is obvious. He is convinced he will meet the alchemist who will impart the final knowledge he needs to complete his production of the Philosopher's Stone. He solicits Santiago's help to try and find him, and in doing so provides the circumstances for Santiago to reach his own next step in his journey toward his treasure: his unexpected meeting at a well with one of the unmarried women of the oasis. Her name is Fatima, and it is love at first sight.

Santiago is instantly more certain than anything in his life that he wants to marry Fatima, and she agrees their destinies are enjoined now forever. They are soulmates, and one day they will be lovers, too, but not until Santiago has been able to continue his journey to discover his treasure. The time for the final consummation of their love is not quite yet, but neither is it far away.

The Englishman finds the alchemist, who tells him to continue his experiments trying to turn lead into gold. Meanwhile Santiago has wandered into the desert to ponder his next steps, when he falls into a trancelike state and experiences a vision.

As he sits under the sun in the desert, he observes two hawks in flight above him. His mind drifts as he watches them and he thinks about Love and The Language of the World, when suddenly one hawk dives to attack the other. An image of a hostile tribal army attacking the oasis passes fleetingly across Santiago's mind. When he awakens, he is so disturbed by the vision that he seeks the counsel of the camel driver. He advises Santiago to approach the tribal chiefs and warn them of an impending attack on the oasis.

At first the oasis chieftains are skeptical of Santiago because he is a stranger. Then the eldest of them recalls the ancient story of Joseph who owned a coat of many colors and, like Santiago, was a stranger in Egypt. Joseph warned Pharaoh that a famine was about to descend on the land and said they should prepare for it. The famine came to pass and Joseph was rewarded by Pharaoh for his vision and warning.

The elders decide Santiago was to be likewise rewarded. He would be given a piece of gold for every ten of their enemies killed if they attacked. But he would die if they did not attack.

As Santiago walks away from the chieftains' tent, the moon is the only light upon his path. He experiences a deep sense of having touched The Soul of the World. Just as he is contemplating the possibility of his own death without any sense of fear, he suddenly encounters the alchemist.

In *The Alchemist* the metaphor of the journey through the desert describes the red phase of Santiago's alchemical process. He has left the white phase behind and now the coagulation of the matter that makes up the highest potential of his personality is being formed. It is out of this potential that his power to perform miracles will be born.

The desert is also a device to introduce the reader to the basics of the world of ancient alchemy, with the comment that Santiago is prepared to be informed about it; but quickly he concludes the physical experimentation approach of the laboratory is not for him. He will leave that to the Englishman, who represents the English and European school of laboratory-based alchemy.

The story of *The Alchemist* is taking us down the road of inner alchemy where intuition, omens and listening to The Soul of the World together make transformation take place.

This is first indicated in the character of the camel driver, whose main skill is reading the environmental elements around him, and his own connection to them.

If the final treasure for Santiago is to be the attainment of powers to bring about a positive change to the world, then being able to speak The Language of The World is essential. His laboratory will be the events of life itself and the world around him. By reading the omens with attentiveness and patience as they appear, he will discover his oneness with everything and become part of the working out of the transformation of all things.

Santiago's Philosopher's Stone will be the fruit of this transformation.

Also worth noting here is that the bulk of Santiago's alchemical experience takes place in what can loosely be referred to culturally as Arabia. Historically Arabs were ultimately responsible for preserving ancient alchemical knowledge. They translated and rewrote many of the ancient Greek myths and academic works, including Aristotle's alchemical instruction book for his student, Alexander the Great. Later there were many Muslim alchemists of renown, and the story names one of them, Geber, as if to make sure we understand their influence.

Arabian alchemy flourished again when Europe was engulfed by the Dark Ages for almost seven hundred years after the fall of Rome. Arab alchemists brought their preserved manuscripts when they crossed from Morocco to Spain in the eighth century. However, these books were full of special jargon and symbolic images which the European intellect took literally and struggled to assimilate. This allusion is also reflected in the Englishman's fixation on turning lead into gold, which ultimately became the direction taken by European alchemists of that era.

(See *Three Arabic Treatises on Alchemy* by Muhammad Bin Umail and M Turab Ali.)

But Santiago recognizes within the culture of the desert the Arabian understanding of the oneness of all things and the importance of omens on the road to transformation.

The story also acknowledges the influence of ancient alchemy in Jewish tradition with the story of Joseph (of the multicolored coat) in Egypt, and his power to dream and interpret those dreams for his own wealth and the common good. Santiago's observation of the hawks and the vision of the future attack on the oasis shows the type of power an ancient alchemist could achieve, and even that of a new one just starting out.

To complete his passing through the red phase, Santiago makes his soulful connection with Fatima. This love at first sight moment between the male and the female is symbolic of the conjunction between the White Queen and the Red King, the moon and the sun in alchemical symbolism. The love Santiago feels towards Fatima is unlike any attraction to a woman he has previously known in that it is not a possessive love; it is given unconditionally. The well within the oasis where they meet is a symbol of a never-ending love of mutual respect and the product of all the hard work of purification and distillation that Santiago has achieved so far. This is mostly a comment about Santiago's inner respect for his inner feminine and masculine and the need for an inner unity, however it is equally true that at some point romantic love between two people needs to mature into unconditional Love if it is to survive.

Yet the love is not yet fully consummated. Santiago has not been able to produce his Philosopher's Stone, but he is about to begin manifesting the power he has discovered so far. He has come a long way and has reached the oasis, which is the symbol of his inner soul. He is now listening to his heart and is open to his intuition.

He is now seeing the world through new eyes; the eyes of his soul, which are connected to The Soul of the World—and which Santiago experiences through his vision. Those hawks are hugely symbolic of the wild and untamed portion of human nature. They are quietly intelligent creatures and will hunt alone and in packs, but they will also fend off another hawk encroaching on their turf because of a food scarcity.

It's hard for those of us who seek peace to admit to this dualistic aspect of our nature, such as fiercely territorial hunter-like aggression on the one hand and peaceful quietness on the other. Yet we see both aspects of this nature played out in the world every day, and we are continually shocked by the destruction that can be wreaked by unbridled human aggression. This dualistic nature of aggression and passivity is innate; for better or for worse, it is the inner seat of all human power. To turn this dualistic nature into a source of positive power is one of the greatest challenges the budding alchemist will face, and it will involve an inner battle.

Taming this power to make it work in our favor and to the benefit of those around us is one of the tests to be faced in the red phase. If only it were as simple as turning off the aggression and turning on the passivity, then there would be no battle. Anyone who has tried to replace all their aggressive thoughts and actions with peace and love toward themselves and others will acknowledge the struggle they face in the attempt.

One option is to opt out of the inner struggle by relinquishing all power and adopting a state of being that is compliant and submissive to all other external power. But this leads to a powerless existence, open to abuse, control and manipulation from others.

The other option is to continually assert our power over others by controlling and attempting to manipulate them to our advantage. But this behavior can quickly become abusive and destructive and never delivers the long term positive outcome we actually want to achieve.

Neither option leads to true empowerment and instead will leave us devoid of the power to perform miracles.

True power is seen when we bring healing, peace and prosperity to the world around us.

The fighting hawks in the story and Santiago's vision of the attack on the oasis are a symbol of this battle for true power.

* * *

Through my own experience of this power struggle in the red phase, I discovered that passivity plays no part in this battle; there will be blood and there will also be gold.

In the previous chapter I described how I discovered a powerful inner child who was at one with The Soul of the World and ready to move forward and play an active role in my adult life. For the first time I felt a sense of inner completeness and harmony. I was at peace with myself. Equally, I was no longer confused about receiving feminine love, which in the past had always appeared unreliable and ready to abandon me at any moment.

In the same way as Santiago discovered unconditional love in Fatima, I could now embrace my own feminine side and move forward into the world, free from needing to constantly define my self-image. I now had a clear goal: to love unconditionally and fulfill my ambitions.

This was a real emotional milestone in my life and an opportunity to break with the thought and behavioral patterns that had prevented me from following my dream and exploring a new direction in life.

I discovered an unknown bravery and a release from fear which I had never known before. Like so many, I had believed my personality was locked in stone and my path through life was "written" and determined by my limitations. Now, to my delight, I found something new was taking place inside me; instead of being an "I can't" person, I wanted to be an "I can" person. My new mantra became: "The world is my oyster and nothing is going to stand in my way."

It would be safe to say that up until this point I could have been labelled a passive or reactive personality rather than a fearless proactive person. I avoided risk and conflict as much as possible and was content to let circumstances dictate my course through life. Up until then, my mindset was clear. Who, I wondered, was I to try and change the outcome of my career, my wealth, my status or my lifestyle? Life is what it is and I should learn to be content with my lot.

But now that I was in the red phase of my alchemical process, I discovered a new outlook emerging from within. I was confident I could determine my future and forge a new pathway ahead. I was prepared to take on a world that had previously seemed totally daunting and full of insurmountable obstacles to a successful career and financial success. But now I possessed a new found confidence, and I was prepared to use it to achieve my dreams.

I instinctively knew this was not going to be a walk in the park. Yet I did not realize how great this challenge was going to be, since I was finally taking on the forces of the world which had long kept me travelling down the road of conformity and passivity. But my passions were rising, as I saw the importance of this do-or-die struggle. I understood, however, that the waters of my Red Sea were not simply going to part because I now wanted to cross into the Promised Land.

The restrictive forces that I had allowed to enslave me in my inner thoughts and outward actions were closing in on powerful chariots, ready to recapture their control. The red phase was going to be marked with death and the red hue of blood to be shed, either mine or that of my captors.

Either way, without any apparent fear, I was ready to risk the death of my old self. I genuinely felt I had nothing to lose. I was determined I was not going backwards to living my old life, because that person no longer existed.

To put this time in my life back into context for a moment, I'd left my career as a teacher in a demanding high school and become a printer. This solitary work had given me the emotional space to complete the black and white phases of my alchemical transformation. But now, in the red phase, I needed the confining door of the print shop to open onto the world and lead to the fulfillment of the new life agenda I had planned.

Love was still my goal, but I wanted to put it to the test in the midst of the cutthroat, competitive environment of the commercial world. I was determined I was going to make money so I could provide for my family. The new life I had planned would involve a new career.

No one in my immediate family had ventured into the world of business, and I had no idea how successful this path would be when I applied for my first job as a publisher's salesperson. It was at this initial stage that I discovered the chariots of my old captors would be permanently at my heels. They manifested as a continuous negative script which was full of reasons why my new course was a bad plan:

"You lack the right kind of experience!"

"You don't have the skills to succeed in sales!"

"You have no idea what you're doing!"

"You will fail!"

"Get back in your box!"

It required all my newfound power to push through those thoughts. There appeared to be no other way to deal with them except to stare them in the eye and answer back:

"Yes I can!"

Ignoring them or trying to reason with them only gave them additional strength. The trick, it seemed, was not to enter into a debate, but rather to destroy them at every turn with only positive responses:

"I have experience of many kinds that will help me be successful!"

"I can quickly learn the additional skills I need!"

"I know exactly what I'm doing!"

"I will not be limited by anyone or anything!"

"I will succeed!"

And so I applied for a sales job. The interview took place during this publishing firm's annual conference, that just happened to be in a major hotel only half an hour from where I lived. I accepted that as omen number one.

I arrived early and was waiting outside the interview room as I watched a stream of highly professional-looking candidates going in to be quizzed for the job. I was the last to be seen, and I sat alone for what seemed like an eternity while I was busy doing battle with my inner chariots of doubt.

Finally, a youngish woman—brunette, with a ponytail and a smiling face—approached me in the foyer where I was sitting. "Hello! Are you Colm? I'm Sarah!"

"Hello, Sarah, nice to meet you!" I had no idea who she was as I stood to shake her hand. But I was grateful that she was so welcoming. Ever so little, I relaxed.

"The team inside have asked me to apologize for keeping you waiting so long. But something urgent has cropped up back at head office and they're in a conference call. Hopefully they won't keep you waiting too much longer." She motioned toward the door of the interview room. "Can I get you something to drink?"

"Thanks, I'm fine." I smiled, hoping that the rest of them were as nice as she was. "But thanks for offering!"

"Have you come far today?" she inquired.

"Actually, I live close by." She was so easy to talk to. "Although it's the first time I've been in this hotel, it seems like a good choice for your conference."

"Yes, it's great, and lucky you for living in such a nice part of the country. I brought my two young girls so they could play on the lovely sandy beach you have here. Do you have family?"

"Yes, a boy and girl, and they love the beach too. I bet your girls are enjoying the warm sunny weather?"

"They're having a fab time and so is their nanny. Which reminds me, I should check to see if they're back in our hotel room. Best of luck with the interview!" She waved goodbye as she sped off in the direction of the hotel elevators.

Wow, I thought: she has a nanny to look after her children? I wondered who she was.

After another ten minutes or so, the door to the interview room opened. I was invited in. I shook hands with the two men in the room as they apologized for the delay and offered me a seat.

"Hello, Colm," one of them began, "I'm Simon, sales director of the firm, and I just got a call from my wife Sarah, who is also our director of children's publishing. She says she's already interviewed you and apparently you're just what we're looking for. She tells me that we should save time and offer you the job!" He laughed. "Who am I to argue with Sarah?"

I smiled. Sarah was the director of children's publishing! I took this as omen number two.

But apparently the interview wasn't over. Simon was looking intently at me. "But I just want to ask you, why we should give this job to a ex-school teacher who has no sales experience?"

Without hesitation, I replied, "Anyone who can sell history

to a class of fifteen-year-old students on a Friday afternoon and keep them engaged, when all they want to do is go home, can sell anything to anyone!"

Simon grinned. "Great answer!" He met the eyes of the other man in the room, and the two nodded in apparent agreement. "When can you start?"

I got the job as a publisher's representative, with a new car and twice my teaching salary. I was now on the frontlines of my commercial battle for financial success. I discovered later there had been twenty highly skilled applicants for the job, and yet they gave it to me—partly because of my positive attitude and partly, I'm sure, because of my serendipitous meeting with Sarah.

I wanted to go into detail about this because it is typical of so many similar episodes that played out at critical moments for the rest of my career. This is confirmation of what we have learned so far in this book: when we follow the alchemical process of transformation, when we are prepared to put in the hard work at each phase and not give up, then all the power of Love will shift the circumstances to make them work in our favor. The Red Sea will part, the chariots of doubt will be destroyed and we will reach the Promised Land.

"A charmed existence!" has often been a phrase many friends have used to describe my amazing life since my passing through the red phase. But what may look like a charmed life on the outside has actually been, inside me, a battle in full swing; in many ways this inner battle was not so dissimilar to the battle in the oasis that took place out of sight in the chieftains' tent in *The Alchemist*.

There is only one solution to the onslaught of negative, obstructive thoughts in the red phase of the alchemical process; they must be engaged in hand-to-hand combat. The power to destroy the thief, who comes in the twilight thoughts as we drift in and out of sleep, derives from the central place within our soul that is strong and confident in the knowledge we are loved. This knowledge can defeat all the negative powers we will now face as we enter the world against the stream of our previous life.

The negativity can live in our existing relationships, our place in the hierarchies of society, our cultural norms, our allegiances, our politics, our belief system: in fact, everything that we have allowed to adversely define our self-worth and identity so far.

* * *

Fortunately, the oasis chiefs did heed Santiago's vision of a surprise attack from the aggressive tribe who were going to break the tradition. The attack came and the oasis survived not by the chiefs passively laying down their arms and surrendering, but by setting a trap for the attackers. Behind the walls of the tent there was bloodshed, with victory for the oasis chiefs. Santiago, as he was promised, was rewarded with gold.

In *The Alchemist*, all of these opposing forces are represented as tribes. The tribes have chiefs and hierarchies. They are constantly warring with each other for food and water. They are neither good nor evil but all require one thing of an individual: unquestioning allegiance to the tribe's tradition and leadership.

The soul longs to transform; society demands that it conform.

In the discipline of sociology, this assimilation into allegiance to the tribe is known as socialization. This is, in summary, an individual's internalization of the norms and ideologies of their society and the means by which a society protects its stability and continuity.

Socialization, as Philip Mayer discusses in *Socialization: The Approach from Social Anthropology*, is also closely connected to developmental psychology: the study of the psychological processes of nature and nurture by which individuals react and respond to the socialization process in their particular culture.

Socialization examines the whole process of learning throughout the life of an individual and how it influences their behavior, beliefs and actions from childhood to adulthood.

All major world cultures and micro-societies (tribes) within those cultures have their distinct and unique influences to bring to the socialization process. They all have one main goal in common despite the wide differences between cultures: to nurture in the individual a positive moral outcome towards the tribe. This is where an individual's views are influenced by the consensus of his or her society. These views are regarded by the society as normal and acceptable to those who are responsible for maintaining society's standards and expectations, such as politicians, teachers, religious leaders, community representatives, parents, peer groups and even the media.

The study of socialization also acknowledges that individuals are not blank slates to be written on by the society they grow up in. Genes or nature also play a part. Genetic studies have shown that a person's society interacts with his or her genotype to influence the behavioral outcome. In other words, sometimes the socialization process delivers the acceptable norm and sometimes not, depending on the genealogical makeup of the individual.

The key point is that societies survive if the majority of people are positively assimilated. As a result, all tribes have spoken and unspoken processes of socialization.

When we are entering into true individual empowerment through the red phase, we will need to learn to deal with the internalized norms of the society in which we live. The question we need to constantly ask is, "Does this requirement of my tribe work for or against my transformation?"

Only you can answer that question in relation to your tribe. Depending on a multitude of factors, in some cases the requirement to conform may suit your transformation needs. But when the societal status quo feels threatened, it will actively endeavor to destroy your attempts at transformation.

For example, during my childhood the attitude toward wealth and riches was absolutely controlled by the socio-economic class in which I was raised. I later discovered that my learned attitude was of no use to my progress toward true empowerment. To the contrary, it was a major disabling force that I have had to continually combat.

Currently there is a lot of negative media comment about the sense of entitlement to money and privilege among the generation of millennials. That may be so. However, as a child of the baby boomer generation, growing up in working class postwar Britain, my experience was the opposite. I had a distinct sense of being unentitled, which had its own set of complex outcomes.

To briefly put this into context, I was born in Britain just seven years after World War II. "The Blitz" bombing of cities during that war had destroyed both my mother's and father's family homes when they were teenagers. Both families lost everything—not just their homes, but all their possessions. The meager insurance they had did not cover acts of war, and so they had to start again with no savings. Even though they were both highly skilled, their work was low paid in those days.

When I was growing up, Britain was still using ration books to control the distribution of essential items such as meat, tea, jam, cookies, breakfast cereals, cheese, eggs, milk and fruit. Gas for cars was rationed until 1950, even though less than five percent of homes had access to a car; this is in contrast to the United States, where at this time every home, on average, had access to at least one car.

During my early childhood, money was very tight for my parents. Even though they both had full time jobs and worked hard, we lived with my grandparents until I was two years old because they could neither afford to rent their own place nor buy a home of their own. I can still remember the first tiny family home we finally moved into, and my father then saving hard to be able to add hot water and an indoor bathroom onto the kitchen. In the 1950s, many working class British homes still had outdoor bathrooms. We were not homeless. We had food on the table and clothes on our backs, but not much more.

Against this social backdrop, I inherited a complex internal script about money, which had many and often conflicting voices. For me, money did not have an objective value and instead was always intertwined with my status in the society in which I grew up. For me, as a child and youth, the value of money was the position it gave my family in society, and in our case this was a fairly lowly position. Money, for me, took on a dualistic significance: out of my envy, wealth was to be despised when it belonged to someone else; and out of fear, poverty was despised because it represented what we were trying to escape. I recall having a distinct sense that we were locked into a low level of wealth, and that this was our lot in life.

Consequently, I never felt that I deserved wealth or was entitled to it in any way. My money ethic was spartan and cheerless: work hard and be grateful you can put a roof over your head and bread on the table.

Consequently, even though I was the first in my family to attend university and enter a profession, money was never my motive. In fact, I was so poorly paid as a high school teacher that I received a low earner's financial rebate to help me pay our house rent from the same local authority that paid my salary. I did not even question this situation.

The point I am making here is that wealth was not something I expected to gain. The socialization process I'd experienced through my family, school and peers left me with an innate resignation that I could not become wealthy. This went on for many years, until I entered the red phase!

Something new started to happen concerning my attitude toward money. For the first time I began to see it in a neutral light and not as an indicator of social status. Not aspiring to achieve wealth was also one of the attitudes I had learned as a way of coping with the disappointment of not being able to reach a standard of living my parents saw other people enjoying. This is where I believe my sense of being unentitled originated, and I had internalized that defense mechanism.

There is no reason, I now thought, why I should be afraid of becoming wealthy. Why not have as much money as possible? I took that conception a step further: Why not have the same lifestyle as the people my parents used to despise? Will they despise me for achieving that? Probably not, I decided.

I chose to change my thinking about money.

Another illustration from my experience I think is helpful here. As I progressed through the red phase and became more aware of my attitudes towards wealth, I also discovered an inner feeling of having been disinherited. The only tangible fact I could hang that sensation on was the financial loss my parents suffered during their time during the last World War. Yet the feeling of having been disinherited from much greater wealth not only persisted but also left me thinking there might be a root cause somewhere deeper within my family heritage. But I had no knowledge of my family history beyond my immediate grandparents. So I decided to start researching whether there was any factual justification for my feelings.

It did not take me long to discover two very important details that explained my sense of losing out on potential inheritance.

On my father's side, my grandfather was abandoned by his father and left in a Victorian poorhouse in Dublin, Ireland, with his mother and brother, and became dependent on the local parish for money and a home, while my great-grandfather lived in a respectable house elsewhere in the city. I have no idea what caused this estrangement but the fact it happened was news to me.

On my mother's side I discovered an even more surprising

story, and it is particularly worthy of retelling for this book. I knew my maternal grandfather was from Leicestershire in England, but nothing more than that. After researching online I located a tiny Leicestershire village which was the home of a family with the same family name four hundred years previously. I also discovered the house they lived in had been preserved. Moreover, it was still lived in by the descendants of those who had purchased it long ago from the people who were potentially my ancestors.

It so happened I was in the region close to the village, on business, at the time of this discovery, and I decided I had nothing to lose in visiting the village and the house. When I arrived I was surprised to find a large and ancient English country manor that I later found out was built in 1620, around the time the first pilgrims arrived in America.

The house was surrounded by acres of farmland and a few village homes that over the centuries would have been built for the farmworkers by the lords of the manor. I parked my car on the gravel driveway in front of the magnificent building and boldly knocked on the old oak door.

Somewhere from the side of the manor a female voice shouted, "Can I help?"

"I'm sorry to bother you," I said as I walked over to greet an elegant lady whose face was framed within a carved stone window frame, one of the lovely details that made this a beautiful building. "Hello!" I greeted her now that we could see each other. She was in the kitchen and holding a potato peeler. "I can see you're busy preparing a meal, but I was in the area and have reason to believe my ancestors may have once owned this house."

"Oh, really!" She stared at me quizzically. "What name?"

"It's Beaumont, my mother's maiden name."

The lady paused for a moment and then turned and shouted at someone inside, "Henry! We've got a Beaumont!" Then turning to me she shouted, "Stay there, we're coming out!"

I walked back to the enormous front door as down the steps came Lady Theresa Pemberton and Sir Henry Pemberton.

"I'm Theresa and this is my husband Henry," she announced as we shook hands.

"I'm Colm Holland, but my mother's name was Beaumont, and from my research our ancestors possibly came from near here."

"Well that may just be the case!" She smiled. "The Beaumonts did own this house. In fact, they built it four hundred years ago. They were a large family. There are dozens of them still scattered around the area. Where are you from?"

I told her the story of my family's more recent whereabouts during my grandparents' time. Again she smiled when I said this was the nearest I could trace their earliest origins.

"Is that your car?" Lady Theresa said, pointing at my car in the drive.

"Yes," I answered, puzzled by the question.

"Jump in! We're going to the village church. There's something you need to see." And then turning to her husband, she barked the order, "Henry, take the potatoes off the stove. We won't be long!"

Lady Theresa marched towards my car and I began to feel I had intruded on their privacy. "I really don't want to disturb your evening," I said. Then I waved goodbye to Sir Henry and followed her to the car, where she was already in the front passenger seat.

As we drove down the manor drive toward the village she peppered me with questions. "Now tell me everything about yourself. Are you married? How many children do you have? Where do they live? What do you do?" I was under friendly interrogation and answered as briefly as I could.

In the car, I could not help feeling, after only a few minutes, that Lady Theresa and I had known each other for much longer.

She explained how the Beaumonts had been the owners of vast areas of the rural county of Leicestershire in the Tudor era, before they sold the house and most of the land to Sir Henry Pemberton's family in 1660. Much of this I already knew, but I also wanted to know why my ancestors sold the estate. I was determined to ask her how Sir Henry's family came to own it. I was still looking for any sign of disinheritance.

We drove through a picture-postcard English village on the perfect summer's evening and parked in the churchyard in the center of a tiny hamlet of houses, surrounded by green pastures for miles around. It was as if I had been transported back in time to a bygone world where the lord of the manor owned everything the eye could see and beyond.

"Your ancestors built the original church and Sir Henry's family maintained it over the centuries. Stay here while I get the key." Lady Theresa ran off to a nearby cottage and left me contemplating what I had discovered.

If this really was my ancestral home, then they had a level of wealth beyond anything I had imagined. "My ancestors were very wealthy?" This was a new thought I was coming to terms with when Lady Theresa returned, unlocked the church door and ushered me into a totally bare, whitewashed interior with no stained glass windows, no paintings and a simple stone altar under the plain east window.

"My guess is the original church was stripped of all its religious icons by Parliament's forces during the English civil war," I commented.

She shook her head. "Actually, no! The story is, your most famous ancestor was a Puritan, and when he built this church it was not that different to what you see now. He was not one for crucifixes or statues of Mother Mary." She smiled and then said, "This is what you need to see." She took another key and opened another door inside the church to a small wooden room known as the vestry.

As I squeezed in past the stacked chairs and boxes, there, in the center of the room, were two life-size stone effigies of a knight in dress armor and a lady in full finery, lying in state. Above them in a small glass frame was the inscription:

"This Alabaster Tomb is that of the Lord of the Manor Sir John Beaumont (died 1621) & Lady Francesca Beaumont (died 1629)."

They lay in the reclined position of devout prayer, and beneath them was the stone tomb that presumably contained their remains. Next to the tomb was a relatively small, two-dimensional stone carving with the depiction of five knights in dress armor, a young lady, and finally, a child wrapped in grave clothes.

"As you can see here," Lady Theresa explained, "Sir John had five sons who lived to adulthood, a daughter who married a local dignitary and another daughter who died soon after birth. My guess is you're descended from one of these sons."

I was in complete shock. I'd come hoping to find some connection to my family's past, but this was more than I ever imagined. There, just inches away from where I stood, were the remains of my ancestors, many generations back, who not only had immense wealth but high social status too.

"Why do you think they sold the estate to the Pembertons?" I asked.

Lady Theresa answered, "The story goes that the gentleman lying here overspent on building the manor house. It's not local stone, but was brought in from the Cotswolds by horse and cart, over one hundred miles away. It must have cost a king's ransom and possibly sent the family bankrupt. Or there's another theory that is slightly more dramatic."

She caught the glint of delightful expectation in my eye and continued, "The eldest son, also called John, who inherited this estate, was also one of the first leaders of the parliamentary revolt against King Charles I. He was a general of the local army whom defeated the king's forces, which led to the king's beheading. Then when the country returned the monarchy under Charles II, John Beaumont was a wanted man, he sold the house and fled to America to join the Puritans there."

She paused as I studied the images of the five sons in the carving.

I picked up on her theme. "So that was probably this first guy on the far left, and if he went to America, that counts him out as my direct line. Which leaves any of these other four from whom I possibly descended. Either way, if the family went bankrupt or some of them had to flee to the New World, my ancestors here might have had to work hard on the land for their existence."

Lady Theresa and I stood together in silent respect as we imagined the possible lives experienced by the people represented before us.

Then she said more. "You should also know you're only the second Beaumont ever to visit and make any enquiries in my lifetime, which is longer than I care to mention. Twenty years ago, an American lady who claimed to be descended from the American branch of your family came on a visit, and I brought her here to see these fine relatives. That would certainly tie into the theory of their needing to flee across the Atlantic. Most of the locals have no idea this tomb even exists, and we keep it locked away to protect it from vandals."

"Thank you, Lady Theresa," I exclaimed. "On behalf of all my relatives who have no idea this tomb exists, I'm extremely grateful for the care your husband's family has taken to preserve the bones of my ancestors. I will do my part to protect them, too, by promising not to put these photos I've just taken on Facebook!"

We both laughed and made our way back to my car. I offered her a lift back to the manor.

"I'll walk, thanks," she replied. "I need to discuss the church coffee morning with the keeper of these keys. Drive safely, and come and visit again any time." She shook my hand and walked off into the hamlet.

As I drove a few miles down the road to the nearest town, something very strange suddenly dawned on me. Forty years earlier, when I was studying at the university not far from here, I was placed in this exact town's school for a few weeks for teacher training. Unbeknownst to me, it was just three miles from my ancestral home! I had been teaching on land previously owned by my ancestors without any knowledge of the fact. I took that as an omen I had discovered something very significant.

I stopped the car in front of the school where I had taught and contemplated what had just happened in the last hour on this warm, midsummer evening. As part of my alchemic red phase I had been actively battling with deep feelings of being disinherited of immense wealth with no real evidence to base those feelings on. Now I had a potential cause that filled in many of the gaps I had open in my feelings. I asked myself if it was possible for me to have a sense in my unconscious caused by events that happened to my ancestors. Can a memory be relayed down my genetic line to my parents and then to me?"

I knew my grandparents on my mother's side very well, and I knew for a fact that there was never any mention of a high society heritage in the family. There was no rumor or story to hang on any notion of loss of great wealth and position. My only clue had been my own sense of loss that had led to me to ask *Love* to show me why I had an attitude to money that included this loss.

My next questions to myself were equally significant. What impact is this sense of loss having on my present attitude towards money? Am I carrying an ancestral grief and resentment that leaves me feeling disempowered? Do I believe in my unconscious that I can never possibly attain the level of wealth my family once had?"

As I sat contemplating where my family had come from four

hundred years ago, my heart was now saying, "Because you have chosen the path of transformation to true empowerment, you will restore your family's fortune tenfold in ways you cannot imagine, not just for your benefit, but that of your descendants. You just need to stay focused on creating your own Philosopher's Stone."

At that moment my heart truly skipped a beat with the anticipation of what lay ahead. I would need a powerful weapon to defeat such a strong sense of disinheritance and to prevent it from being an ongoing trend within my future.

No more loss of wealth was my goal!

To achieve it, my experience of the red phase was covered in the blood of all the dead negative thoughts within as I slayed them, one by one.

Transformation towards true empowerment can, if we choose it, include achieving financial prosperity. Money may be neutral, but it is also a form of power. It holds power because it is an enabling means of generating beneficial conditions for those within our sphere of influence.

Freedom from hunger, disease, slavery and homelessness are just some of the obvious benefits that money can bring when its power is used for good. And of course, the converse is true when the pursuit of wealth creates destructive results. Yet because Love wants us to transform towards true empowerment, the power we need to create wealth is at our disposal.

If we choose to include wealth among the outcomes of our empowerment, Love will open the way to make it happen so long as we are prepared to fight the inner battles against the doubts and attitudes that want to rob us of that power. Remember, Santiago walked away from the battle in the oasis with gold in his pouch; the same can be true for us too.

We just need to stay focused on creating our own Philosopher's Stone.

The weapon I use every time I hear or sense in my thoughts

and feelings any insecurity about wealth and security, is to name it as a lie and repeat a mantra from the words attributed to Jesus of Nazareth:

"And he said unto them; Take heed what ye hear: with what measure ye mete, it shall be measured to you: and unto you that hear shall more be given. For he that hath, to him shall be given: and he that hath not, from him shall be taken even that which he hath."
(Mark 4.24-25.)

For Your Consideration

The red phase is about the conception of the true self, the unity of the inner male and female powers taking on the world and defeating the enemies within. At this point you can enter into the newfound power you discovered in the black and the white phases of your alchemical transformation. Love is on hand, inspiring and guiding you to identify and defeat the inner negativity that would hold you back from entering into your true empowerment.

In my example, I have focused on my relationship to money and wealth. Money may not be an issue for you. But the process I have discussed of recognizing negativity can equally apply to any other destructive area of your life.

You may battle with chronic self-doubt around relationships or romantic love and friendships. You may have voices within that say you cannot possibly hope for a happy life in that regard and need to settle with second best. This is a lie, of course; if you discover these voices in your white phase, you will now need to face them head on during the negative attack in the red phase. These thoughts will need to be destroyed. Remember, don't try to reason with them or make compromises. Death to negativity is the only answer to finding the gold of fulfillment.

You may have doubts about your creativity. But the same principle applies: as you progress through the black and the white phases, you will reach a realistic assessment of your skills and talents and your ability to fulfill the dream of a creative life. It may not look the way you imagined, but it will happen if you are prepared to put in the hard work and let Love lead the way.

The obstacles standing in your way include the negative forces of your tribe that will possibly present a host of reasons why your dream cannot come true. Some of these you may have already internalized, and others will attack in real time. Either way, these thoughts are the enemy and must be destroyed. Remember to show no mercy!

The context and details of your individual red phase are unique to you. Your challenges and battles with negativity can only be fought and won by you.

The good news is that in the past these inner destructive forces would have seemed undefeatable; now they can be conquered. You will be the victor and move on with the prize of fulfilling your dreams.

This battle is not for the fainthearted. But you will discover that in those places where you thought you had the heart of a lamb, ready for the slaughter, you now have the courage of a lion, ready to devour every opportunity.

Before we move on, I want to briefly consider the concept of opportunity. A major lesson within the story of Santiago and his ability to understand the meaning of the vision of the hawks was the opportunity afforded him to gain riches from following the omen. Because he acted on the vision and used it to the benefit of the oasis in which he lived, he had the gold for the next stage of his journey.

An opportunity to transform will present itself at the right moment. If you have the eyes to see it and act upon it, then the result will bring you treasure. The story I told earlier about my first job in sales is an example of what appeared to be a relatively easy opportunity in my career. Yet in reality it required a lot of my inner work to be able to manifest the benefit it presented.

When I knew what I wanted, the inner work I had invested in transformation put me in alignment with the opportunity

An opportunity can appear when you have all the ingredients in place. It will happen when you are committed to the inner work of transformation, with a clear goal in mind, and you have the eyes of your heart open to see the omen when it appears.

I urge you to dig deep and find the courage to face all your inner enemies, those thoughts that stand in the way of your alchemical progress and want to rob you of your dreams. As you read this, know that I have asked Love to provide you with the right opportunity at this point in your life, so that everything you want will come to pass.

Chapter 9

The Alchemist

In the preceding three chapters, I have discussed the importance of the black, white and red phases in the alchemical process. Each stage in this process is essential to achieving the goal of creating the Philosopher's Stone. In this chapter I will outline the penultimate stage toward the desired treasure of true empowerment.

It should be noted that this next stage is not as clearly outlined as all the other stages in ancient alchemy. This is because it is not so much about a process, but instead about the persons involved in the process. It is about the alchemists themselves and their generational heritage which has been passed down through the ages. It is also about understanding the ancient alchemists' caution about how they shared their knowledge.

I am not suggesting for a moment there is a secret society of alchemists that we need to join. If it exists, then I am completely unaware of it, and as Groucho Marx said, "I wouldn't want to belong to a club that would have me as a member!"

Although this stage is much less dramatic than joining a covert group, it is no less exciting. There does seem to be a requirement for an alignment with, or an acknowledgement of, support from another alchemist who has previously worked through the alchemical process.

This seems to be true no matter how independently we approach the activity of transformation; we need an encounter with an alchemist to complete the process. The reasons for this will become clear as we explore in brief detail the lineage of some of the ancient Arabian alchemists in particular.

* * *

In today's world of logic, reason and science, how do we make contact again with the teachings of the ancient alchemists? Where can we be inspired by the insights and secrets they held? *The Alchemist* is the most widely read revelation of the principles revealed in the Emerald Tablet and the most significant relationship in the story is between Santiago and the alchemist, with the latter appearing at exactly the right moment he was needed by the former.

In the story, as the desert caravan pulls into the oasis, the arrival of Santiago and the Englishman is being watched by the alchemist. We are made privy to his thoughts: he's seen the great and the poor alike pass through the desert and arrive at the oasis because he's been around for a long time; his preoccupation at that moment is to discover the one person the omens have told him he needs to help through conveying the "Language of the World." He ponders why this must occur through the alchemical process of word of mouth rather than written or some other communication. The important inference is that only life itself can ultimately teach what the alchemist's apprentice needs. It is his important job as an alchemist to offer Santiago the final encouragement to take the last step in reaching his true destiny, and to do so in person.

Not long after Santiago leaves the chiefs' tent after sharing his vision of the surprise attack, he considers that in consequence he faces either death, if his warning was unjustified, or gold if he was right. What he realizes is he is no longer afraid of death. His time in the desert has freed him of that. This has been his greatest fear, and now he is able to look death in the eye without fear. It is at this moment that the alchemist appears to him.

Santiago immediately assumes he is the enemy, looking to kill him because he has warned the chiefs of their imminent attack.

The alchemist confronts Santiago by challenging his courage, determination and focus. Santiago stands firm before the powerful show of force from the alchemist, who invites Santiago to visit him — that is, if he is still alive by sunset.

Santiago survives the day and now has enough gold to complete his journey to the pyramids. As previously agreed, Santiago visits the alchemist and asks why he wanted to see him. The alchemist reveals that he received an omen from the wind to help him, and immediately Santiago assumes that is how he will receive instructions about what he should do next to find his treasure.

Instead, the alchemist explains he is not going to give any instructions. But he does invite Santiago to go into the desert with him the next day: there is one important test the alchemist needs to make to see if Santiago is ready to fulfill his destiny. He asks Santiago to find life in the desert using his own intuition. The alchemist needs to know if Santiago can read the desert. If he can, then he will take him as his apprentice.

Santiago passes the test by watching his horse's reaction to a hole under a rock. The alchemist reaches into the hole and pulls out a cobra. This was the omen the alchemist needed. Santiago is now the alchemist's apprentice.

The alchemist questions Santiago to see how badly he wants to find his ultimate treasure. He discovers, however, that Santiago already is prepared to settle for what he has: Fatima and some gold, rather than the greater treasure that could still be his. In reply, the alchemist makes it clear that while there is no harm in Santiago being grateful for what he has achieved so far, it pales into insignificance to the treasure that awaits him. He points out that Santiago has lost sight of his true ambition; one day that loss of enthusiasm will catch up with him and leave him, like so many dreamers, never receiving the true reward for all his efforts. The alchemist also hints there is a chance of time running out if Santiago procrastinates too long; there is a real danger of never finding his treasure. But if Santiago is determined to find his treasure, the alchemist will go with him on the journey.

Santiago considers all his work and the risks he has taken

so far. Contrary to his recently articulated resolve, he listens to his heart and decides to go with the alchemist into the desert toward the pyramids. If he does not attempt this final step, he will never know if the treasure exists. He will face the danger of running into warring tribes; he will venture away from the safety of the oasis and his new-found love with Fatima. Now, he decides, while the alchemist is offering to help, is the time to seize the day.

The question is, what does Santiago gain from his time with the alchemist?

As the alchemist leads Santiago on this journey across the desert, he takes the opportunity not only to remind Santiago of what he already knows about alchemy but also to help him listen to the most important voice in his life: his heart! The lesson he wants Santiago to remember most is that he can never escape his heart, so his best advice is to listen to it. The ultimate goal of the apprentice alchemist is a unity of heart and mind, which in turn will lead to action.

As he crosses the desert for the next seven days, the alchemist helps Santiago to listen to his heart and eventually learn to accept it for the way it is—sometimes afraid of pain, occasionally complaining, but never silent. The alchemist tells him that actually the heart's fear of suffering is worse than the suffering it will experience. That is why, says the alchemist, we cannot always rely on our hearts to encourage us when we want to push beyond the comfort of what we have.

Santiago learns to let his heart have a voice, but then speaks back to it when it lacks courage. In fact, under the tutelage of the alchemist, he tells his heart not to be afraid, because God and eternity are leading the way in his search for his treasure. At this point, Santiago's heart confesses to know all about dreams and treasure and agrees with Santiago that he is on the right path. The alchemist finally nods. He has been waiting for Santiago to reach this place of inner unity, where his heart is joined with the "Soul of the World" to help him reach his dream. Just at the point when most people give up, Santiago's heart could now guide him toward his real treasure.

In this part of the story, the alchemist represents the school of Arabian alchemy that Jung, too, had affirmed. Earlier in the story, that Arabian connection had been mentioned by the Englishman when he first met Santiago. A friend who had been on an archeological dig, according to the Englishman, had heard about an alchemist with miraculous powers. He was said to be two hundred years old, had visited Europe, could turn lead into gold and had discovered the Philosopher's Stone. We can infer the alchemist in the story is representative of this Arabian tradition stretching back all the way to Thoth himself.

The lesson here is that everything Santiago has learned and worked hard to achieve on his path to true empowerment has led him to a level of maturity that is repeatedly tested by his interactions in this story. His success in interpreting the behavior of the hawks and his discovery of the cobra is evidence of this. The story is sending a very clear message here: all the reading, listening to experts, speaking to other travelers, counselling sessions, self-analysis, and even following our dreams can only be of value if we can live it out in the real world of our day to day life in society and nature. Moment to moment we need to be able to interpret the omens that Love brings to us through the "Language of the World."

Alchemy is not a theory or religion. It is not a philosophy or a therapy. It is about living life to the full in the world, with all its surprises, disappointments, victories, defeats, challenges and rewards. Alchemy is not another world we can escape to. It does not offer an illusionary existence or paranormal state. Alchemy makes us engage with life with all the pain and joy that it brings. Our destiny, the alchemist teaches us in the story, is as much about the process as it is about finding the treasure. We also have the reassurance of knowing we are not alone. Love will underpin us and be at the heart of all we do.

Santiago learns from the alchemist that he simply needs to dare to live in the light of the knowledge he has gained so far. He can find support from Love by simply contemplating a grain of sand or watching the path of a meteorite. He simply needs the eyes to see and the ears to hear. Alchemy teaches us how to see and hear; it gives us the skills to dig deep into the power of life that lives in all things. It enables us to find the courage to face the fear of death.

The alchemist also represents the final encouragement we need to push us through any lingering doubts about carrying on to the final stage. Love will send that encouragement at the critical moments we need it. The actions of the alchemist reveal an important truth in the makeup and nature of that encouragement. It's akin to the encouragement given by a parachute instructor as they order you to jump out of the plane, rather than someone saying: "Would you like to jump?" It is less like the kindly aunt who offers candy when we cut a knee in sport, and more like the older brother who drags us by the collar back into the rough of the game. Dare I suggest that it may even be found in the most unexpected forms, such as the bully who challenges us to defy him and is shocked when we push past and ignore him. In other words, it is the encouragement to face our final and worst fears and not let them stop us from moving forward.

The character of the alchemist embodies the part of Love that draws from us the courage and determination to carry on, whatever the consequences, against our deepest dread. This is what the ancient alchemists understood, together with the need for it to be actualized by a real person.

The alchemist, in person, must point us in the direction of our real treasure.

The alchemist is like a mentor or, similarly in Christianity, a godparent at a child's baptism. It is a slightly vague role but undeniably essential to completion of our alchemical apprenticeship. The alchemist is there at a deciding moment: at the crossroads when we are assessing our next step, usually when we are at the brink of giving up and stopping the search for our real treasure.

Finally, there is another, less clear but critical role the alchemist plays in the final stage of our transformation. In my study of the story of *The Alchemist* and my research into ancient alchemy, I am convinced this is possibly the most important event in reaching our real treasure.

We will need the alchemist to perform an act of "invocation" on our behalf.

Only when we have connected with the alchemist in our story, and he has spoken to Love on our behalf, will we be able to perform miracles. Why is this the case? Because the alchemist invokes what we already know so we can pass through the great test, as we will see in the next chapter.

In my preface, we discovered how I found *The Alchemist* and the consequent meeting with the author, Paulo Coelho. I described how Paulo had asked God, what was the best thank you gift he could give me? Paulo knew nothing about me, except I was the Australian sales and marketing director for his book, and I had been inspired to order a large quantity based on my first reading of his manuscript.

At that meeting he said that God told him to spend a day in prayer asking the universe to give me what I most wanted — and all I needed to do was decide what that was! In other words, he worked with Love for me to be able perform the miracle of manifesting whatever I wanted.

This was what I call my own "alchemist moment," made all the more significant because at that time I had no knowledge of alchemy and no realization that, up until that point, the inner and outer transformation I had been pursuing for most of my life followed the principles of the alchemical process.

In tandem with this reality was the fact that Paulo, too, had no knowledge of any of this. He was simply grateful for my intuition about the future success of his book. He believed that I'd listened to my heart, and in turn, he listened to Love to know the best gift he could give me. I am grateful every day that he did.

Until I later returned to study *The Alchemist*, I also had no idea that the story clearly illustrates in detail the importance of this alchemist moment.

The alchemist's role is to help us question our hearts, because as Jesus of Nazareth said: "For where your treasure is, there will your heart be also." (Matt. 6.21) In the context of Matthew's Gospel, it's a moral instruction about not focusing on material things to the exclusion of the spiritual. However, even divorced from the gospel context, this is still a truism: our heart and our treasure can be found in the same place, so the fulfilled life is one in which our mind and our heart are aligned in unison of purpose.

Here was my dilemma when I met the alchemist. I was grateful for the treasure I had discovered through my life. As we have seen in previous chapters, I had worked hard in every way I could—spiritually, emotionally and practically—to achieve some specific goals with success. I had found Love, I was blessed with a happy family and I had a career that paid the bills.

These were all amazing achievements, and I celebrated them with gratitude and humility. Yet I could still hear a voice deep within, and the voice said: "But..."

Yes, I had found my life's companion. But would my wife accept my need to fulfill all my ultimate ambitions?

I had a happy family. But now wanted to take a financial risk.

I got the job I was looking for, but I really wanted my own business.

I asked myself, where is this "but" coming from?

Eventually, I found the answer by listening again to my heart.

If it is true that our heart always knows where our treasure is and we reach the point of discovering our gold, then our heart will know that. If we have truly learned to listen to our heart and we can't hear it saying "but," then it is time for celebration. There will be a deep, abiding knowing that we have reached a place of true empowerment in our life, and this will be confirmed by our ability to perform miracles.

The alchemist is the catalyst for us to enter into the final phase of our alchemical process, where we can move into action and manifest the power to produce gold, create priceless treasure, fulfill all our dreams and perform miracles.

Beware, however, of one crucial lesson to be drawn from *The Alchemist*: we may have stopped listening to our heart when we can no longer hear it screaming the word, "But...!"

Love has inspired our hearts to want the best for our lives. When we have achieved the integration of our mind and our heart, then miracles happen.

This was the point of my alchemist moment. This was the point when my life shifted to a new dimension; and as I moved forward and listened to my heart, endless miracles began to take place.

I was ready for the final stage of the alchemical process, where all this can be manifested—as I will outline in the next chapter of this book.

For Your Consideration

Because you are committed to transformation, Love will send the alchemist into your life, and at exactly the right moment. Congratulations! When the alchemist comes into your world, it means you have reached an advanced stage in your transformation. You are finally living joyously in the reality of life with the unity of your heart and mind.

The alchemist will be more than a mentor. He or she will be the encouragement you need to help you keep pushing beyond the point of giving up. Your alchemist will help you take the final step to perform miracles on your own.

Most likely, your alchemist will be a stranger up to the moment of your first meeting. Your alchemist will be sent by Love at the perfect moment and will know what to do on your behalf. This is how the alchemical process has survived down through the millennia, since the beginning. There is no traceable or recorded lineage to track the line from the first alchemists to you, but the incredible truth is—at this moment, you are part of that chain.

You are part of the oldest process in which humans have been conscious of their creative role in the scheme of the cosmos.

But of course, you know all this because you are in tune with your heart and Love.

You are free to accept the alchemist's assistance or ignore it. But there will be no doubt when the alchemist moment takes place. Your alchemist will identify herself or himself to you, and there will be a genuine engagement of purpose between you.

There is no formula to the process of this relationship. It can be fleeting, as it was in my case, or it can last as long as is needed; but it will end at some point.

You are unique and your individual alchemical process belongs to you under the guidance of Love. I must, however, add a word of caution. The relationship will only happen once in your lifetime! It will be a single event, and you will know when the encounter is happening.

There will never be a string of alchemists knocking on your door asking to help you, so it is critical to pay close attention to the moment and to be conscious that you need to act upon it to be able to move forward.

What happens between you and the alchemist will be perfectly tailored by Love. One thing is certain: the alchemist will have the exact wisdom you need to complete your transformation. You may initially ignore what the alchemist offers, yet it will be the perfect knowledge for your final transformation stage. Whether you act upon the wisdom immediately or further on in your life will be your choice and will become a matter between you and your heart. If you continue to ignore it, then as the alchemist says to Santiago, eventually you will give up on your journey toward your real treasure; and it will be too late for you.

If you accept the alchemist's help, then they will perform the invocation with the cosmos and Love that is uniquely for you.

The final good news is that Love will bring the alchemist into your life to invoke what you already know; as you act upon that wisdom, you are ready for the great test.

Chapter 10

The Great Test and Transfiguration

The ultimate goal of the ancient alchemists working in the laboratory was to be able to create the Philosopher's Stone. This was so they could align any substance into the ideal form they had in mind for it. In other words, whatever they would bring out of their own consciousness.

Perfection of a substance was what they sought, and the Philosopher's Stone could deliver that. It could heal and turn matter into gold. "Chemicalization" is the name the alchemists gave to this ultimate skill of being able to consciously project or manifest their desires into being. Chemicalization referred not just to the object that was being changed but to the alchemist who was changed. This was the great test of an alchemist's skill, and very few were successful in achieving it. (For more on this, see Marie-Louise Von Franz, *Alchemy: An Introduction to the Symbolism and the Psychology*.)

Of course, we now realize the Philosopher's Stone *is* the alchemist.

The power to change, to manifest something out of nothing, to transform the worthless into something valuable, lies within the alchemist. The alchemists were engaged in inner transformation over the ages, so they could bring about a similar change in their world. This is why they worked so hard to reach this point.

This is where real miracles happen!

It is worthwhile restating some important principles about how the alchemists, and even modern scientists, view their ability to control the nature of matter; and the best place to do this is quantum physics.

Quantum physics, otherwise known as quantum mechanics or quantum theory, maintains that all matter is made up of quanta—packets of energy. These were discovered during scientific efforts to understand the nature of light.

Richard Feynman, one of the founders of quantum theory, and winner of the Nobel Prize for Physics in 1965, commented, "I think I can safely say that nobody understands quantum theory." (See *Surely You're Joking Mr Feynman: Adventures of a Curious Character*, by Richard P Feynman and Edward Hutchings.)

It is safe to say that our mechanical concept of reality, as described by scientists such as Newton, was incomplete until the early 20th Century. Then what eminent physicists during the era of Einstein discovered was, contrary to our perception, the world is not solid and unchanging. Instead, it is continuously being reformed from a chaotic quantum energy that is guided by our expectation of what is there. For example, in the case of light, physicists concluded that it is made up of both waves and particles of energy at the same time. Einstein argued that this could be explained if light was composed of bundles, or photons. A photon carries energy proportional to the wave frequency of the speed of light but has no mass that can be measured when it is not in motion. (See Malcolm Longair's *Quantum Concepts in Physics: An Alternative Approach to the Understanding of Quantum Mechanics*.)

The discovery of photons played a key role in the founding of quantum physics. It was the study of the photon's properties that opened up the new class of fundamental particles called quantum particles. Thanks to photons, we know that all quantum particles have both the properties of waves and particles. We also know that energy can be discreetly measured on a quantum scale. This was the beginning of the quantum revolution.

Central to this new understanding of matter is the role of the human observer. Put simply, the way that matter behaves, including light, is relative to the viewpoint of the individual observing it. This is at the heart of Einstein's Special Theory of Relatively in which he describes the constant speed of light, and that it is impossible to determine whether or not you are moving without looking at another object. Without the involvement of the observer, the activity of light is meaningless.

The amazing fact is that all of these modern concepts of matter are at the heart of ancient alchemical beliefs, but very few quantum physicists give credit to the influence of alchemy upon their early defining theories. An exception is Wolfgang Pauli, an Austrian-born theoretical physicist who died in 1958 but whose life's work was to mathematically prove Jung's theory that human consciousness could influence physical matter.

Pauli was driven by an unshakable belief that the thoughts of the scientist will directly affect the outcome of an experiment. Like Einstein, he wanted to prove that there was a "Grand Unifying Theory" behind everything in the universe; he included human consciousness as one of the components in the theory. The term "The Pauli Effect" was even given to a phenomenon experienced by all scientists, when their equipment fails due to the anticipation of the failure in their own minds. (See *The Interpretation of Nature and the Psyche,* by Carl Gustav Jung and Wolfgang Ernst Pauli.)

On a less anecdotal level, Pauli is credited with numerous groundbreaking discoveries of theoretical subatomic particles which significantly advanced the development of quantum physics. His theory of "Electron Spin" provided a mathematical means of identifying invisible particles known as "bosons". More than fifty years after Pauli's death, other scientists were awarded the Nobel Prize for building on his research, which was in turn inspired through Pauli's study of alchemy.

Most significantly, Pauli's "Grand Unified Theory" has seen further experiments like the ones carried out recently at Upton, New York. Physicists at the RHIC (Relativistic Heavy Ion Collider) are studying the primordial form of matter that existed in the universe shortly after the Big Bang. Using both lead and gold ions, they have created a liquid-like substance called "quark-gluon plasma" or "quark soup" for short, a perfectly dense fluid that exists at temperatures greater than those on our sun. The hypothesis, widely accepted from these experiments, is that this "quark soup" is the force that holds together all the atoms that make up our world. (For more on this, see Mario Campelli's *Inside Cern's Large Hadron Collider: From the Proton to the Higgs Boson*.)

It is reasonable to assume that what the ancient alchemists called the prima materia is in fact the same conceptual substance that scientists now call "quark soup" and everything that exists contains this.

If the latest science agrees there is an indivisible connection between everything in the universe, then the ability of the observer to affect a change to matter is not as outlandish as previously thought. Jung and Pauli deserve our thanks for re-establishing our understanding of the power we possess, and the process of chemicalization is worthy of our study.

It should be noted that this process was only ever attempted by experienced and devoted alchemists who had already passed through all the previous alchemical disciplines I have outlined so far. These ancient alchemists reached the point where they were ready to face what I call the great test (my term for chemicalization) and bring about change through the power they had developed.

What the alchemists discovered through the great test is that if they followed a specific process they could directly and positively affect the outcome of a situation or change the nature of matter. In other words, they could perform miracles (and I use the term miracles in the Christian understanding, in which something positive and life giving happens without any visible or natural cause.)

There are several versions recorded in ancient alchemical writings of the great test. These can be roughly summarized into four key stages, which were the inner processes required of the ancient alchemist before they could manifest their desired thoughts into being. (See Arthur Edward Waite's *The Secret Tradition in Alchemy*.)

Stage one was called "saturation." This was the initial focusing of the alchemist's will or intent upon the outcome to be manifested. This is human will in its purest form: the unwavering decision to follow a specific outcome driven by the deepest commitment and all the passion the soul can muster.

This passion was sometimes referred to as the inner "secret fire," and many alchemists down through the ages tried to describe this most mysterious of powers. Some said it was the life force of the alchemist, that can just as easily destroy as it can create. Many alchemists thought that this inner fire was so powerful that only those who have control over their own shadow self can be told how that power can be aroused from within.

To disguise its true nature in their writings, alchemists have referred to it symbolically as a sword or various hunting weapons. In Greek mythology, it is the fire Prometheus stole from heaven or that Vulcan used to form the thunderbolts of Jupiter in Roman mythology. Whatever it is, and however they describe it, the alchemists all agreed that without the secret fire there could be no miracles.

The second part of the process was "combustion." Put simply, this is where the alchemist's will was focused without other distractions and with the intention concentrated on a desired outcome. It often helped the alchemists to imagine their minds as sealed containers in which this thought experiment would take place. It was sealed to prevent any outside interference entering the container, while at the same time being able to release any impurities or negativity with such a controlled process.

This was regarded as a particularly difficult activity for even the most experienced alchemists, and ultimately required the giving of the whole self to the process. Learning how to deal with the negative waste produced by the thought experiment was essential to prevent any unwanted interference. Combustion continued for as long as was needed to bring the object focused on to the boil or climax.

As soon as the peak of combustion was reached, it was immediately followed by silence. This is the third stage, where the alchemist completely withdrew the inner secret fire from the process, and a state of total thought silence was maintained. The alchemist then divested themself of all investment in the desired outcome, while at the same time not losing the core intent. During this period of silence the power of intent from the alchemist had been unleashed into the cosmos, and was given time to work in harmony with the first matter that unites all things, to bring about the desired outcome.

During the great test, the ancient alchemists were often tempted to feel that their work had failed, and yet they refused to let despair take over. The trick, it seemed, was mastering the art of letting go without giving up, which was a delicate balance essential for success.

The fourth and final stage was "realization". This was regarded as the part requiring a bridling of the natural tendency toward exuberance. More will power was now needed to control the desire to artificially manipulate or manufacture external conditions to produce the desired success.

Patience with action, that identifies and follows the omens, is the key ingredient and virtue at this point. If the alchemist followed all the previous steps correctly, then the manifestation happened in good time. The intent became a reality, but not always immediately or obviously, and especially not necessarily in the way or form that was originally expected.

The miracle happened when the alchemist acted upon the intent as if it had already come to pass in a state of calm contentment, with the purest joy rather than in a burst of external delight. The balance was to move forward in the knowledge the work had been done, without impatience or undue force. The intent manifested naturally and in harmony with the world and the heart of the alchemist.

Of course, all the effort of these stages was fruitless unless the alchemist reached the realization that she or he is made of the same first matter as the rest of the world, and the thoughts and heart of the alchemist are the connection to that great truth. The alchemist who became one with the spirit within all things was the one who could perform miracles.

* * *

In *The Alchemist*, Santiago is ready for the great test. He's accepted the assistance the alchemist has offered, and is ready to face his first opportunity to put his new found power into practice. This will be his final step before he reaches the pyramids and his treasure. He has come a long way, and he is going to need to draw upon everything he has learned so far to bring his quest to a conclusion.

They've crossed the desert for seven days and are preparing to go their separate ways when the alchemist tells Santiago one last thing he needs to know before he can fulfill his dream. He will be tested by the world so he can master everything he has understood so far, and he warns this is the point at which most apprentice alchemists give up.

The alchemist tells Santiago that the test will be severe, and Santiago reaches into his heart to consider whether he is ready for such an ordeal. His heart reminds him of the courage and enthusiasm he has displayed so far and how his heart has protected him from danger even when he was unaware. On that basis, Santiago decides he and his heart are ready for the final test, whatever that might be, and he pushes on with the alchemist toward the pyramids.

Death was always Santiago's greatest fear, and this fear is

justified as they ride into the middle of a large group of warrior tribesman who take Santiago and the alchemist into captivity. When they are asked by the tribal chief to explain why they are wandering in a war torn desert, the alchemist gives a strange answer. Instead of saying he is an alchemist, he introduces Santiago as an alchemist who possesses power over nature and, furthermore, adds that Santiago wants to demonstrate this power to the chief.

The alchemist then gives Santiago's gold coins to the chief and offers up their lives if Santiago does not destroy the warriors' camp using only the wind within three days.

This is the great test for Santiago, and there are only two possible outcomes: success or death. Santiago has no idea how to turn himself into the wind. On the first day he spends his time trying to come to terms with his new found situation: he has lost his life's savings and is now looking death in the eye.

On the second day he climbs a cliff where he can commune with the desert and listen to his heart.

On the third day he is joined on the cliff by the alchemist and the tribesmen who are eager to see Santiago destroy the camp by just using the wind. They settle down to watch as Santiago speaks to the desert from his heart.

Santiago now enters into his first alchemical great test. He has already learned to let his heart lead the conversation with the desert, the wind and the sun.

The main topic of their conversation is Love. The conversation between the natural elements and Santiago is the climax of all he has learned throughout the story and is the most illuminating episode in the book.

Santiago explains to the desert that Love is the link between all things and how life exists in everything; in return the desert offers up its sand.

Santiago then helps the wind to see it knows nothing about Love, but if it did, then it could do more than it ever had before and turn a man into the wind. The wind responds by covering the sun with the desert's sand, so Santiago can look into the heavens.

The sun learns from Santiago that its understanding of Love is also limited; it is full of contemplation but no action. He explains that humans are the secret ingredient in all the world, because they bring Love through action to enrich creation. The sun concedes Santiago's wisdom, and advises him if he wants to become the wind to speak to the hand who wrote all.

The focus and intent of Santiago's thought projection experiment was to become the wind. That way, he could show the tribal chief he had power over nature, and then the chief would spare his life and Santiago could complete his journey to the pyramids. There he could claim his treasure and return to Fatima, whom he loved.

Love was his ultimate intent, and this is the lesson of this episode in the story. Each element of nature: the desert, the wind, and the sun, all tested this intent and discovered it was truly Love driving Santiago's pleas for help.

Santiago now prays to the hand who wrote all, but it is not a conversation as such. This is no longer a prayer for help but a prayer of realization of the ultimate truth. Santiago reaches a climactic moment of understanding—only Love can perform miracles, and Love lives within everything that exists because Love created everything. He concludes that if Love also lives within his own heart, then he, Santiago, can perform miracles through his actions.

At this point in the story, the wind blows, the tribal camp is almost destroyed and Santiago is miraculously transported from the cliff to the other side of the camp. As a result of all this, the chief releases Santiago and the alchemist so they can continue their journey.

Santiago has successfully completed his great test, and now he can step into action and follow the omens toward his final goal: to find the treasure and return to Fatima.

It is not a great leap to compare the story of Santiago on the cliff, being watched by the alchemist and the desert tribe, to the transfiguration of Jesus of Nazareth, as he was watched by his disciples, in the story in the New Testament. Similarly, it can even be likened to Moses receiving the Ten Commandments from God on Mount Sinai in the Old Testament, with the tribe of Israel waiting on the plain below.

Moses was enveloped in a cloud out of which God spoke, and Jesus' disciples heard God's voice telling them that Jesus was his Son and they should pay close attention to everything he said. In both cases the writers of the Old and New Testament are trying to make a very important point, which is that Love and human beings need not be separated. They can be united in purpose.

Love lives within the soul of all of nature but uniquely is active in each of our hearts.

We are the agents of Love in the world when we choose transformation. Even more importantly, when we follow the alchemical process there will be a point where we will become conscious of that truth in a way that I describe as transfiguration.

Carl Jung says in his book *Alchemical Studies:* "...the divine process of change manifests itself to our human understanding and how man experiences it—as punishment, torment, death and transfiguration."

In my experience, Jung is correct. As we have seen throughout this book, when we follow the path of change it will mean facing death in the form of our worst fears. But the reward is the experience of transfiguration, in which we know we are at one with Love and can perform miracles through action.

I only enter into the great test when I believe the omens are pointing to the need for one, because it must be initiated by Love. It will also require every ounce of my own power. For the sake of privacy I am not going to share the specific details but I will outline the main steps involved.

It starts with the principle in the prayer by the American theologian Reinhold Niebuhr:

"God, grant me the serenity to accept the things I cannot change,
Courage to change the things I can,
And wisdom to know the difference."
(From Essential Reinhold Niebuhr: Selected Essays and Addresses.)

The point is that alchemists are not magicians with magic wands that they wave around on a whim to make everything work to their favor. An alchemist can, through the great test, perform miracles of real importance that will improve the wellbeing of their life and those in their world.

An omen will tell me if I can change something or not, and this is a critical first step. I must know in my heart if the situation I think needs to be changed can indeed be improved. Quite often the first indication that I need to perform the great test is a concern that begins to dominate my mind and then my heart.

This can come from a thought or be just an enduring sense; or something someone says; or even just my observation of a situation. I need to have a conviction that Love wants to act to make things better in some way. It can be anything that needs transformation to a better state for me or for someone else: a lifestyle situation, an emotional trauma, a personal predicament or perhaps a physical ailment.

The world is full of things that cannot be changed and many that can; in the words of Niebuhr's prayer, I need to know the difference.

I will carry the concern for as long as it takes by looking for the omens to encourage me to believe the situation can be improved by way of a miracle. The key omen I am usually looking for is a stated intent for transformation toward an improved state of wellbeing, either within my own heart if the situation involves me, or in the person Love has brought to my concern. Almost always if it is on behalf of someone else, it is because they are known and close to me or Love has brought them across my path for a reason.

Then Love and my heart will help me make the final decision. If the decision is: "No! This situation cannot be changed at this time," then I do not disregard it completely; instead, I park it in a place reserved in my heart for later, when the time may be right. If the answer is, "Yes! This situation can be transformed at this time," then I get to work straightaway.

For the stages of the great test, I follow the process of chemicalization as I outlined earlier. I usually conduct the experiment by using the time when I am in bed at night, before sleep, and then again as soon as I wake or even in the night, if my sleep has been interrupted. This can continue for at least three nights or for as long as two weeks, as needed.

Saturation Phase: I use my deepest imaginative skills. To start, I visualize the person(s) involved, and I surround them in a gold circle of light. Then I ask Love to envelop them to help me exclude all other distractions. This can happen quickly or can take a few attempts, depending on how easily I am able to focus on the person.

Not until I am able to maintain a continuous focus do I then begin to think about what transformation is required. I am concentrating on their stated intent, in which they are committed to a change but need support to make it happen. For example, if I am helping someone move on emotionally, I will think first about the hurdles they are facing currently and what needs to change for them to be able to move to a new place of wellbeing. As well as being highly focused on the present and visualizing the future, I am also listening for clues to the deeper causes of their dilemma.

Sometimes the cause may be something they are completely unaware of, and yet it is sometimes revealed to me. I take mental note of these causes and write them down later in a notebook. I should say that sometimes when I am doing this work, I may drift in and out of sleep; this is perfectly normal and means I am working in the optimum space between my conscious and unconscious.

Combustion Phase: This is where I increase my concentration on the person within my imaginary gold circle by bringing the heat of my secret fire through my full intent for the desired transformation to take place. All other distractions, thoughts, feelings and concerns have been banished from my imagination. I have created a world within the space between my conscious and unconscious; a dream-like reality where I am helping the person create the intended outcome in their soul before it can be manifested in their daily life.

Specifically, I am working to bring healing or change to the causes preventing transformation as they are revealed during the work. If I see a wounded child that needs to know love and nurturing, I imagine Love caring for that child. If I discover hereditary traits that are holding back the person in his or her life now, I put those in an adjoining gold circle and let Love give them what they need to let go of their influence. I cannot move on until I am satisfied all of the blocks have been identified.

For the next step I imagine Love as a ball of light, constantly flowing around the gold circles in a figure eight, moving ever faster and enfolding the person in the purest grace and benevolence of the cosmos. I imagine Love within all things and within me coming to the aid of the person and even those negative influences in the adjoining circle, if there is one.

This is the great test.

It is exceptionally difficult to achieve and has taken me years to perfect. Each time I perform this experiment, this part always requires every ounce of my own heart's focus to be successful. In the early years of my work with this, I would have to revisit this point several times over, for many days before I knew this stage of combustion was done.

Silence Phase: This is not so much the absence of activity but more the withdrawal of my passion for the outcome in the process. This is no time for a rest as there are still some jobs to be done. Firstly, if there are any negative forces in the adjoining gold circle they need to be cut free to return to their place and time of origin; that is necessary because now they are free of their need to exert their influence on the person. They have been met by Love, and I often visualize a cutting of any bonds that attach them to the person; together we watch them drift away in peace, with my blessings as well as the blessings of the person being released.

Next, I let the light of Love continue its quiet process of assimilating the prima materia of the person with that of the cosmos, so that the circumstances of his or her life and those of the world around them slowly align to bring about the desired outcome. I have no control over this, and in many ways my work is done. I am now a humble observer who must wait in silence without being able to affect or know how the transformation will unfold. My sole function is to hold the intent unwaveringly with patience.

Realization Phase: The period of silence can extend for a few hours each day until I have a deep reassurance that the main part of the great test is complete and I enter the final stage of Realization. This is where there is no longer any need for the imaginary work. I am fully back into the daily consciousness of reality, with the joy of knowing that Love has already brought the transformation of the person's soul into being.

Now I just need to be patient and watch as it manifests into their day-to-day life. The skill needed here is to give up having any investment in the outcome while still holding on to the intent. The only active role I can engage in without attempting to manipulate and influence the outcome is to fill my heart with gratitude. I am grateful that Love is in control and the best result will eventually unfold. In my experience this can occur in hours, days, weeks, months or even years. One thing is certain. It will come to pass, and it will be full of Love and wellbeing.

For Your Consideration

This is in many ways the crunch point of this book. The great test is potentially one of the hardest activities you will engage in during your lifetime, and it is made all the more challenging because the outcome will not always appear in the form you necessarily expect. But take heart because it will always be miraculous and it will always be engulfed by Love.

By way of encouragement, I want to simply say that passing through the great test will always include transfiguration for you, too, and is therefore the most sublime human experience known to anyone who has followed the way of the ancient alchemists. It will be painful and it will be exalting beyond any other experience you have ever known. The outcome will be a new existence, in which seeing miracles will become a way of life. The miraculous will be commonplace, because Love and your inner being have become one.

The challenge of the great test now stands before you, and you are the only one who can commit to enter into it alone. But take heart in the knowledge that while it may be a path less travelled, many great people have walked this way before you. They will be watching and, just as the alchemist watched Santiago, they will be there in your work. Your reward will be that moment of transfiguration, and to that end, by way of encouragement, I want to leave you with this story.

On a very ordinary street corner in Louisville in Kentucky there is a very unusual cast-iron plaque set into the ground. It reads:

"A Revelation: Thomas Merton had a sudden insight at this corner Mar. 18, 1958, that led him to redefine his monastic identity with

greater involvement in social justice issues. He was 'suddenly overwhelmed with the realization that I loved all these people...' He found them walking around shining like the sun."
(Quotation from Merton's *Conjectures of a Guilty Bystander,* pages 140-142.)

What the plaque commemorates is on that day in 1958, Thomas Merton had a life changing revelation, or perhaps we can say, a transfiguration moment, which happened not in the isolation of his inner work but as a result of years of contemplative prayer and solitude. In his mind, each person around him was glowing like the sun, as transfigured beings. He suddenly saw the interconnectedness of all people as if a veil had been lifted from his eyes, and he experienced only Love for all he saw. It was not so much that he had "arrived" in his oneness with Love, but rather had just begun and the result was action. He spent the rest of his life working for the unity on earth that he had experienced in his transfiguration moment.

This is why you have come this far, so you can move on to live an empowered life of action driven by Love. Remember, I have called on Love to provide everything you need as you pass through the great test. And there is nothing to fear.

Chapter 11

Action

Throughout this book I have continually focused on the primary purpose of the *magnum opus* or great work of the ancient alchemists, which put simply is the eventual manifestation of true empowerment.

In this final chapter I want to explore how we can manifest that power through action in our daily lives and change the world around us in a positive way — and in particular in the creation of the two most important elements of wealth and wellbeing.

I want to acknowledge the multiple levels of empowerment that we can naturally experience throughout our lives, beginning in childhood. The child who is loved and nurtured to maturity will normally manifest personal empowerment in a strong and positive way. Ideally, those responsible for their upbringing have encouraged the child to explore, question and understand the world around them to the point where they are free, as far as is possible in their society, to think for themselves and act with self-awareness. They become people who know their own minds, and they want to act to improve the world they live in for the greater good.

Ideally they will have access to quality education to acquire all the skills and knowledge they need to lead a fulfilled and selfless life to the benefit of others. They are truly empowered. I say ideally because that should be the case for all children, but it is heartbreaking that according to UNICEF, fifty-nine million primary school aged children across the globe are not in school, and thirty-eight million more leave primary school without learning to read, write and do basic arithmetic.

This is compounded in many instances by wretched living conditions, where the lack of clean water and sanitation bring an early death from preventable diseases and where war, famine and abuse prevent children from having even a basic chance of survival. What chance do these children have to even begin to live a fulfilled life? Where can they find the opportunity to overcome the seemingly insurmountable barriers they face?

Of course, part of the answer is that those who have the power to help change their circumstances can act to provide at least the right environment for them to flourish and enjoy fulfilled lives. So why has that not happened, given all the hundreds of years of wealth and prosperity around the globe? What is stopping those who have the wherewithal from acting to help empower those who do not?

There are a million and one reasons why not, and one core issue at the heart of the matter also has to do with the lack of true empowerment. The fact is that even children who are raised in seemingly ideal circumstances are more often than not disempowered by a multitude of factors as I have described through this book and in examples from my own experience. I had a good education and was nurtured to the best ability of my parents and teachers. But as we have seen, the degree to which I had the emotional ability to help myself and those I love was seriously hampered along the way. That was why I chose transformation and the alchemical process — so I could discover true empowerment.

As we have seen throughout this book, the history of the ancient alchemists shows the human spirit has longed to transform and create the Philosopher's Stone so they can miraculously heal and bring prosperity to the world. I have tried to illustrate the amazing impact that has made.

In and through the process of creating our Philosopher's Stone, miracles naturally begin to happen. Even just the action of committing to transformation sees the beginning of positive and often life enhancing events and experiences.

History is also full of examples of famous alchemists bringing what seems to be miraculous progress to the world of medicine and science. For example, it is worth looking at the work of Dr. Paracelsus who is revered as a pioneer of medicine in 16th Century Renaissance Europe. Born in Switzerland and educated at the best universities of that time, he displayed extraordinary medical skills that have secured him a place in medical history.

At the time, Paracelsus was well-known for his talent through his repeated curing of one of his contemporaries, the well-known printer, Johann Froben in Basel, Switzerland, which caught the attention of great humanist scholar and teacher, Erasmus. (Philip Ball's *The Devil's Doctor: Paracelsus and the World of Renaissance Magic and Science* expands on this.)

The humanist Erasmus and Paracelsus struck up a friendship at the University of Basil, where they both lectured, and their correspondence about medicine and theology lasted a lifetime. Paracelsus is remembered for his contribution to modern medical techniques such as the treatment of syphilis, which was almost at epidemic levels at the time, and his realization that epilepsy was a disease and not the result of demonic possession.

Probably his most significant work was in the field of antisepsis, where he showed other doctors that keeping wounds clean and allowing nature to heal itself would save lives, rather than applying the foul concoctions commonly used at the time. He was also one of the first physicians to realize that poor environmental conditions contributed to creating ill health, such as dust and poisonous vapor found in children's working conditions.

What has been so often forgotten—or conveniently overlooked—in the history of Paracelsus' great achievements is his devotion to alchemy and his belief in its basic principle of first matter. He even used the name *archeus*, a term commonly used by the alchemists to describe the ability of nature to heal itself, and this is obviously the same principle referred to as the Soul of the World in *The Alchemist*. What Paracelsus was trying to identify is a source of health that inhabits all matter, including the human body.

This physician was no charlatan; in fact, he continually denounced the proliferation of fake cures and superstitions being peddled across Europe. His contribution to advances in medicine is just one historic example of where alchemical principles have been at the center of the theories that have changed all of our lives for the better.

Modern medical science did not spring out of nowhere; it evolved from the fundamental understanding of nature and the interconnectedness of all things that is at the heart of ancient alchemy. The transformation from sickness to health is one of the purposes of creating the Philosopher's Stone.

In the same way that modern medicine has been influenced time and again by the principles of ancient alchemy, the freedom to create wealth and the currency of money to trade that wealth originates from the alchemical concept of transformation. Money is simply an agent of transformation in our global financial structure, and therefore the creation of wealth through money can result in true empowerment. Money, as the currency in our societies which can bring about change from poverty to wellbeing cannot be ignored. Indeed, it must be embraced and actively pursued to bring about the welfare of the societies in which we live. This is another purpose of the Philosopher's Stone; it turns lead into gold.

The freedom to pursue health and wealth is equally important. It is easy to take for granted the freedom enjoyed by our modern civilization, and we can forget it has been hard won by pioneers down through the ages who have fought against tyranny, dictatorship, corruption, greed and violence. From the beginning of ancient alchemy, the freedom to do good has been a core motivation for transformation. There can be no transformation toward the power to do harm to others; that is a contradiction in terms. The desire to hurt or destroy others is the antithesis of transformation and is driven by fear.

The insight we will discover as part of our alchemical process is that money is in itself neutral; it is neither good nor evil. It is what we do with that money that decides the power it has.

Of course, the ability to create wealth is not the sole prerogative of the alchemical process. It is open to everyone, and again the success in the pursuit of making money is no respecter of motive or person. The good and the bad can make money. Everyone can engage in endeavors to make money out of any motive such as fear and greed or hope and selflessness; however, none of these motives guarantees a greater degree of success.

What characterizes the ancient alchemists in their pursuit of wealth is their motive and intent within the alchemical process. *The Secret of the Alchemist* is the process they used to create wealth with the encompassing motive of bringing wellbeing into their sphere of influence. This is wonderfully illustrated through one of the famous fathers of modern chemistry, the 8th Century Arab alchemist Jabir ibn Hayyan. (See *Names, Natures and Things: The Alchemists Jabir ibn Hayyan and his Kitab al-Ahjar (Book of Stones* by Syed Nomanul Haq.)

Many types of now basic chemical laboratory equipment and commonplace chemical processes are attributed to Jabir ibn Hayyan. He is also one of the first chemists to identify substances such as citric acid and mercury. Most historians also agree that his primary contribution to both chemistry and ancient alchemy is documenting his process of experimentation. His work on the classification of elements was groundbreaking, even though it may now seem primitive. He identified substances that he called "spirits" because they evaporated upon heating; solid objects that could melt he called "metals" and he named as "powders" those non-malleable stones that would not evaporate or melt.

As an alchemist, Jabir ibn Hayyan was not just fascinated with what we now call chemistry and the discovery of the component elements of all matter. He was also ultimately driven by the ability to create gold itself because it was the currency of wealth in his era, as it still is today. Perhaps most importantly, his aim was to observe and document the process needed to make gold from base metals.

Although this record does not exist in a way we can actually understand. He did not want his knowledge to fall into the hands of those who would use it for evil purposes, so he hid his wisdom within over five hundred books. "The purpose is to baffle and lead into error everyone except those whom God loves and provides for," he wrote. He is also believed to be one of the first writers to use the concept of steganography, where the true meaning is only available to the initiated within other writings.

For centuries, various scholars (including those translated in *The Arabic Works of Jabir ibn Hayyan,* edited by E.J. Holmyard) have eventually deciphered the essential steps that Jabir ibn Hayyan believed an alchemist must bring to each experiment to transmute base metal into gold.

Following, based on my reading of his work, is my summary understanding of the beliefs that Jabir ibn Hayyan used to describe these inner processes.

All things are one: Everything is comprised and connected by the unseen and original *Prima Materia.*

Thoughts can create matter: The alchemist's thoughts can influence the creation of gold from base matter.

Harmony with the Soul of the World: Positive creativity, not greed, must be the underlying motive.

The heart must be grateful: Fear of want must be banished by gratitude for plenty in the heart of the alchemist.

The total focus must be on the creation of gold: Front and center of the alchemist's mind must be constantly on the creation of wealth.

Working with the natural world: The alchemist must understand the natural processes of how all things have their own natural transformation.

Nothing is created without action: Miracles do not happen by accident; they are the result of the alchemist's action.

Action is, as we have already discovered, the one unique ingredient that humans alone can bring to the world to make it a better place. When human action is inspired and powered by Love, then the whole of nature, seen and unseen, is enriched. That enrichment can be manifested in numerous ways, including the generation of wealth. The ancient alchemists knew that if they followed these essential steps, they would be able to create gold.

* * *

In the story of *The Alchemist*, Santiago has reached the point where he is empowered to move into action to discover his treasure. The alchemist tells him that action is driven by an understanding that this imperfect material world is a reflection of the unseen, perfect world, and when we grasp that truth we can tap into Love's power and bring change to this world.

He then tells Santiago he is now only a few miles from the pyramids and the riches he seeks. All Santiago has to do is make the final steps to get there. He has come a long way, and this is the final action he must take. His dream is within reach, and he has one action left to perform. To find it, he must start digging.

Santiago sets off alone and very soon he sees the pyramids for the first time. His heart is full, and tears of joy fall onto the desert sand. He sees a scarab beetle on the ground where he is kneeling. A scarab beetle is the same insect the Egyptians believed represented good fortune. (It is also the same beetle Jung captured in his study and had appeared in his patient's dream, enabling him to help her acknowledge her unconscious feelings.) Santiago also rightly takes the beetle as an omen and starts to dig for his treasure on that very spot.

We know the outcome. Santiago is ambushed by thieves, and there is no treasure to be found in the sand. But he is told where to find it. The treasure is back where he first had his dream, under the sycamore tree in Andalusia. Battered almost to the point of death, he slowly makes his way home via the monastery where the alchemist has left him some money for the journey.

Back in Spain, Santiago sits under the sycamore tree and contemplates his journey back to the point where he first began. The lesson he specifically draws to mind is the importance of following the omens. Doing it guaranteed his success, and the treasure was now his. He digs and sure enough, there is a chest full of more than enough treasure to pay the Gypsy woman and then rejoin Fatima at the oasis: only this time, he would not have to leave her alone again.

Santiago had performed a miracle, and he attributed it to using the alchemical process: listen to your dreams, follow the omens, commit to transformation, face your greatest fears, invoke the power of Love in all things and take action to make it finally happen. When he walked that path, he discovered the greatest truth of all: Love is there, giving generously, because Santiago wanted true empowerment and to love unconditionally.

* * *

When I was close to completion of the final manuscript of this book, I was looking for a story from my life to conclude with, and it just happened to be my birthday. I was invited to my five-year-old grandson's house. He informed me I would have a cake with candles, and then we would play a treasure hunt he had solely devised, without any help from his parents. The cake was produced, and he helped me blow out the candles. But before we could eat, we had to play the treasure hunt.

As you can imagine, my attention was already focused on the word "treasure", but even more so when he produced a small map with clues to follow. I was stunned again when looking at the map. It included finding a golden pyramid!

"Come on, Papa, we have to find the treasure!" He pulled me up from my seat, and we made our way around the house, finding drawings of arrows he had made in various rooms, which eventually brought us to the stairs in the entrance hallway. Under the stairs was a cupboard. The last arrow he had drawn pointed to the door of the cupboard.

"What does this mean?" I asked.

"You have to go in the cupboard under the stairs to find the treasure, Papa! The stairs are the golden pyramid, and this is a secret door into it. The treasure is in there!" His excitement was rising. He ordered, "Go on, then! Get in the cupboard!"

As I looked at the cupboard, tears rose to my eyes. I was recalling the cupboard under the stairs where my mother shut me in the darkness—and where my own inner child once lived, feeling punished and powerless.

I gently opened the door and, just when I realized there did not seem to be any treasure in the darkness, I felt a gentle push from behind.

"Go in, Papa and you'll find the treasure!"

"Yes, but it's very small and dark in here," I replied. "How will I find it?"

"Just use the torch on your phone," came the very practical reply.

So I crawled in using the light on my mobile. There, at the very back of the cupboard, on a small piece of paper, was a drawing in orange crayon of what looked like a skeleton.

"I think I've found it!" I shouted from deep inside the cupboard. "Can I come out?"

"Yes, and now we can eat the birthday cake" he replied with a tone of voice that intimated the job was done.

I crawled out and joined the family at the dining table and I showed everyone my newly-found treasure. "What exactly," I asked my grandson, "is this drawing?"

"It's a golden skeleton from ancient Egypt, and it's priceless!" he explained.

"Wow! Thank you!" I replied. "Should we put this in the British Museum?"

"No," came his reply, "it's yours to keep forever!"

He looked at me somewhat oddly, as he could see I was eating my birthday cake with teary eyes full of happiness. I gave him a big thank you hug for the best birthday gift I had ever been given—and a story that sums up everything I have wanted to say in this book.

The Secret of The Alchemist is easy to understand when you have the eyes to see it.

The dream comes from the wounded child within. It is this child that holds the answer to finding our greatest treasure. As we shine the light of Love into that darkest of places, we can help the child to take the action to find true empowerment.

The child can often be found in the cupboard of my life, when I am challenged to move forward and have to face my greatest fears. My child's initial reaction seems always to be feelings of self-pity and powerlessness. And yet, as my adult self brings the light of Love and the alchemical process to the situation, the child enters into true empowerment and leads the way to producing the treasured outcome; miracles happen.

I just have to follow the omens that Love provides; amazingly, they are always there in abundance, if I just have the eyes to see them and accept the task of taking the action toward wellbeing and wealth.

For Your Consideration

This is the last chapter of *The Secret of The Alchemist,* and I want to remind you of a promise I made at the beginning of this book. The moment you commit to transformation, you will see an improvement in your personal power, if you really want it. As you complete this book and apply each insight, you will move forward to live a life full of true empowerment.

How do I know? This is the promise I made to you, the reader: "I have asked Love to give you everything you need so that whatever you want will come to pass. All you need is to decide what you want."

This is a good moment to ask you the question again, "Do you know what you want?"

You may even find that your original answer to that question has changed as you have been reading this book. There is no right answer, but it does need to be full of truth and honesty.

You may not like the answer, and you must be careful not to judge it or suppress it. Full and open acceptance of what you truly want is required before the dream can be fulfilled. If the answer includes the desire to transform toward true empowerment, then you can use all the power of the alchemical process to make it come to pass.

In the words of St Francis of Assisi, "Start by doing what is necessary; then do what is possible; and suddenly you are doing the impossible."

Answering the question, "What do you want?" is necessary before we can proceed to transformation. The answer you give will also indicate the stage of the alchemical process you may be at. For example, if the answer is "I want to overcome my fear of making myself vulnerable to others," then it may indicate you need to visit the child within and bring Love into the memories that are making you ashamed or fearful of the power of those feelings.

If the answer is, "I want to be financially successful," then you may need to consider your inner relationship to money and address any attitudes or blocks that are hindering your progress toward financial wellbeing.

Whatever answer you give to the question— "What do I really want?"—will reveal your heart's dream, and this is where your treasure lies. The alchemical process of transformation will enable you to fulfill your dreams with the help of Love.

How do I know this will be true for you?

By now, I think you know the answer to that question!

You are the alchemist in your world, and Love will make it happen.

Further Reading

Campbell, Joseph. *Reflections on the Art of Living, A Joseph Campbell Companion*. Selected and Edited by Diane K. Osbon. First Edition. New York: HarperCollins Publishers, 1991.

Coelho, Paulo. *The Supreme Gift*. Adapted from Henry Drummond's sermon: "The Greatest Thing in The World." Barcelona: Sant Jordi Asociados, 2013.

Johnson, Robert A. *He—Understanding Masculine Psychology*. New York: HarperCollins Publishers, 1989.

— *She—Understanding Feminine Psychology*. New York: HarperCollins Publishers, 1989.

Julian of Norwich, *Revelations of Divine Love*. Translated by Barry Windeatt. Oxford World Classics. Oxford: Oxford University Press, 2015.

Lachman, Gary. *Jung the Mystic, The Esoteric Dimensions of Carl Jung's Life and Teachings*. New York: Penguin Books, 2013.

Levy, Paul. *The Quantum Revelation, A Radical Synthesis of Science and Spirituality*. New York: Select Books, 2018.

Peck, M. Scott. *The Road Less Travelled*. New York: Random House, 1983.

Powell, John. *Why Am I Afraid to Love?* Mexico City: Argos Communications, 1967.

Bibliography

Ball, Philip. *The Devil's Doctor: Paracelsus and the World of Renaissance Magic and Science.* New York: Random House, 2014.

Brown, Robert McAfee, editor. *Essential Reinhold Niebuhr: Selected Essays and Addresses.* New Edition. New Haven, CT: Yale University Press, 1987.

Campanelli, Mario. *Inside Cern's Large Hadron Collider: From the Proton to The Higgs Boson.* Singapore: World Scientific Publications, 2015.

Campbell, Joseph. *The Hero with a Thousand Faces.* Third Edition. Novato, CA: New World Library, 2008.

— *The Inner Reaches of Outer Space.* Perennial Library. New York: Harper & Row, 1988.

Coelho, Paulo. *The Alchemist.* New York: HarperCollins, 1993.

— *The Pilgrimage.* New York: HarperCollins, 1995.

Clymer, R. Swinburne. *Hermetic Science and Alchemical Process.* Whitefish, MT: Kessinger Legacy Reprints, 2010.

Dyer, Wayne W. *Real Magic.* New York: HarperCollins, 1992.

Feynman, Richard P. and Edward Hutchings. Surely You're Joking Mr. Feynman: Adventures of a Curious Character. London: Vintage Books, 2004.

Holmyward, E.J., editor. *The Arabic Works of Jabir ibn Hayyan.* Translated by Richard Russel in 1678. New York: E.P. Dutton, 1928.

Jaffé, Aniela, editor. *Memories, Dreams, Reflections by C.G. Jung.* New York: Random House, 1965.

John of the Cross, Saint. *Dark Night of the Soul.* Translated by E. Allison Peers. Chicago: Dover Publications Inc., 2003.

Johnson, Robert A. *Owning Your Own Shadow: Understanding the Dark Side of the Psyche.* San Francisco, HarperSanFrancisco, 1991.

Jung, C.J. *Alchemical Studies*. Vol. 13 *Collected Works by C.G. Jung*, Edited and Translated by Gerard Adler & R. F. C. Hull. Princeton, NJ: Princeton University Press, 1983

— *Aion: Researches into the Phenomenology of the Self*, Vol. 9 Part II, *The Collected Works of C.G. Jung*. Edited and Translated by Gerard Adler & R. F. C. Hull. Princeton, NJ: Princeton University Press, 1979.

— *Archetypes and the Collective Unconscious*. Part I of Vol. 9, *The Collected Works of C. G. Jung*. *Psychology and Alchemy*. Volume 12, *Collected Works of C.G. Jung*, Edited and Translated by Gerard Adler & R. F. C. Hull. Princeton, NJ: Princeton University Press, 1980.

— *Psychology and Alchemy*. Vol.12, *Collected Works of C.G. Jung*. Edited and Translated by Gerard Adler & R. F. C. Hull. Princeton, NJ: Princeton University Press, 1980.

— *The Structure and Dynamics of the Psyche*. Vol. 12, *Collected Works of C.G. Jung*. Third Edition. Edited and Translated by Gerard Adler & R. F. C. Hull. Princeton, NJ: Princeton University Press, 1975.

— *Symbols of Transformation*. Vol. 5, *The Collected Works of C. G. Jung*. Edited and Translated by Gerard Adler & R. F. C. Hull. Princeton, NJ: Princeton University Press, 1976.

— *Synchronicity: An Acausal Connecting Principle*. Volume 8. Collected Works of C.G. Jung. Edited and Translated by Gerard Adler & R. F. C. Hull. Princeton, NJ: Princeton University Press, 2010.

Jung, C.G. and Wolfgang Ernst Pauli. *The Interpretation of Nature and the Psyche*. Introduced and translated by Marvin Jan Greenberg. New York & Tokyo: Ishi Press, 2012.

Kirsch, Thomas and George Hogensen, editors. *The Red Book. Reflections on C.G. Jung's* Liber Novus. London: Routledge, 2014.

Longair, Malcolm. *Quantum Concepts in Physics: An Alternative Approach to the Understanding of Quantum Mechanics.*

Cambridge: Cambridge University Press, 2013.

Maxwell-Stuart, P.G. *The Chemical Choir: A History of Alchemy.* London: Continuum International Publishing Group, 2008.

Mayer, Philip, editor. *Socialization: The Approach from Social Anthropology.* London: Routledge, 1970.

McGrath, Alister E. *Christian Theology, An Introduction.* Fifth Edition. Hoboken, NJ: Wiley Blackwell, 2011.

Merton, Thomas. *Conjectures of a Guilty Bystander.* New York: Doubleday, 1966.

— *Contemplative Prayer.* London: Darton Longman & Todd. 2005.

Moore, Robert L. *Facing the Dragon: Confronting Personal and Spiritual Grandosity.* Asheville, NC: Chiron Publications, 2003.

Newton, Isaac. *Keynes MS. 28. The Chymistry of Isaac Newton.* William R Newman, editor. Bloomington, IA: Indiana University, 2010.

Nomanul Haq, Syed. *Names, Natures and Things: The Alchemist Jabir ibn Hayyan and His Kitab al-Ahjar* (Book of Stones). Boston Studies in the Philosophy of Science. Dordrecht: Kluwer Academic Publishers, 1994.

Pinch, Geraldine. *A Guide to the Gods, Goddesses and Traditions of Ancient Egypt.* Oxford: Oxford University Press, 2002.

Schwartz-Salant, Nathan, editor and introduction. *Jung and Alchemy.* Princeton, NJ: Princeton University Press, 1995.

Shakespeare, William. *The Winter's Tale.* London: First Folio, 1623.

Umail, Muhammad Bin an M. Turab Ali. *Three Arabic Treatises on Alchemy.* Whitefish, MT: Kessinger Legacy Reprints, 2010.

Von Franz, Marie-Louise. *Alchemy*: An Introduction to Symbolism and the Psychology. Studies in Jungian Psychology. Toronto: Inner City Books, 1982.

Waite, Arthur Edward. *The Secret Tradition in Alchemy.* Routledge Edition. London: Routledge, 2007.

Wheeler, Philip N. and Hans W. Nintzel. Alchemical Symbols:

Volume 21. The R.A.M.S. Library of Alchemy. Santa Monica, CA: RAMS Publishing Company, 2015.

Note to reader

Thank you for purchasing *The Secret of The Alchemist*. For information about online courses and events go to: http:// colmholland.com

Sincerely, Colm Holland

BOOKS

SPIRITUALITY

O is a symbol of the world, of oneness and unity; this eye represents knowledge and insight. We publish titles on general spirituality and living a spiritual life. We aim to inform and help you on your own journey in this life.

If you have enjoyed this book, why not tell other readers by posting a review on your preferred book site?

Recent bestsellers from O-Books are:

Heart of Tantric Sex

Diana Richardson

Revealing Eastern secrets of deep love and intimacy to Western couples.

Paperback: 978-1-90381-637-0 ebook: 978-1-84694-637-0

Crystal Prescriptions

The A-Z guide to over 1,200 symptoms and their healing crystals

Judy Hall

The first in the popular series of eight books, this handy little guide is packed as tight as a pill-bottle with crystal remedies for ailments.

Paperback: 978-1-90504-740-6 ebook: 978-1-84694-629-5

Thinker's Guide to God
Peter Vardy
An introduction to key issues in the philosophy of religion.
Paperback: 978-1-90381-622-6

Your Simple Path
Find Happiness in every step
Ian Tucker
A guide to helping us reconnect with what is really important in our lives.
Paperback: 978-1-78279-349-6 ebook: 978-1-78279-348-9

365 Days of Wisdom
Daily Messages To Inspire You Through The Year
Dadi Janki
Daily messages which cool the mind, warm the heart and guide you along your journey.
Paperback: 978-1-84694-863-3 ebook: 978-1-84694-864-0

Body of Wisdom
Women's Spiritual Power and How it Serves
Hilary Hart
Bringing together the dreams and experiences of women across the world with today's most visionary spiritual teachers.
Paperback: 978-1-78099-696-7 ebook: 978-1-78099-695-0

Dying to Be Free
From Enforced Secrecy to Near Death to True Transformation
Hannah Robinson
After an unexpected accident and near-death experience, Hannah Robinson found herself radically transforming her life, while a remarkable new insight altered her relationship with her father, a practising Catholic priest.
Paperback: 978-1-78535-254-6 ebook: 978-1-78535-255-3

The Ecology of the Soul
A Manual of Peace, Power and Personal Growth for Real People
in the Real World
Aidan Walker
Balance your own inner Ecology of the Soul to regain your
natural state of peace, power and wellbeing.
Paperback: 978-1-78279-850-7 ebook: 978-1-78279-849-1

Not I, Not other than I
The Life and Teachings of Russel Williams
Steve Taylor, Russel Williams
The miraculous life and inspiring teachings of one of the World's
greatest living Sages.
Paperback: 978-1-78279-729-6 ebook: 978-1-78279-728-9

On the Other Side of Love
A woman's unconventional journey towards wisdom
Muriel Maufroy
When life has lost all meaning, what do you do?
Paperback: 978-1-78535-281-2 ebook: 978-1-78535-282-9

Practicing A Course In Miracles
A translation of the Workbook in plain language, with mentor's
notes
Elizabeth A. Cronkhite
The practical second and third volumes of The Plain-Language
A Course In Miracles.
Paperback: 978-1-84694-403-1 ebook: 978-1-78099-072-9

Quantum Bliss

The Quantum Mechanics of Happiness, Abundance, and Health
George S. Mentz
Quantum Bliss is the breakthrough summary of success and
spirituality secrets that customers have been waiting for.
Paperback: 978-1-78535-203-4 ebook: 978-1-78535-204-1

The Upside Down Mountain

Mags MacKean
A must-read for anyone weary of chasing success and happiness
– one woman's inspirational journey swapping the uphill slog for
the downhill slope.
Paperback: 978-1-78535-171-6 ebook: 978-1-78535-172-3

Your Personal Tuning Fork

The Endocrine System
Deborah Bates
Discover your body's health secret, the endocrine system, and
'twang' your way to sustainable health!
Paperback: 978-1-84694-503-8 ebook: 978-1-78099-697-4

Readers of ebooks can buy or view any of these bestsellers by
clicking on the live link in the title. Most titles are published
in paperback and as an ebook. Paperbacks are available in
traditional bookshops. Both print and ebook formats are
available online.

Find more titles and sign up to our readers' newsletter at
http://www.johnhuntpublishing.com/mind-body-spirit

Follow us on Facebook at https://www.facebook.com/OBooks/
and Twitter at https://twitter.com/obooks